Sophie Conran
The Mini Book

This book :

. . . .

THE MINI BOOK OF

Pies

SOPHIE CONRAN

HARPER

To my little guinea pigs,
Felix and Coco
Love Mummy

Contents

INTRODUCTION

What is a pie? Sounds like a simple question, but over the years pies have been and still are many varied things, so for a definition I'd say the looser the better. Pies can be savoury or sweet, enclosed or open, with pastry or not, the right way up or even upside down. Pies helpfully are often called a pie, but sometimes it's a pasty, a quiche, pudding, tart or even a cake.

Big or small, pies are wonderfully difficult to define. The term "pie" is used to describe dishes that aren't pies at all but confections, and their adjunct can describe their filling or not. An Eskimo pie is my favourite offender, being neither a pie nor containing a single shred of Eskimo. It is, in fact, an oblong of ice cream covered in chocolate. So, in keeping with the rebellious nature of pies everywhere, I've sneaked some controversial ones into this book!

Pies have been the food of kings and of paupers, eaten at extravagant banquets or taken down Cornish tin mines (the origin of the pasty), and there was a time when the streets of every town across the land would have been filled with the shouts of pie sellers. Yet in recent years the reputation of pies has suffered greatly in the public imagination, largely due to the many food crimes committed in its name. Pies have become associated with unhealthy, mass-produced snacks made from the otherwise unwanted parts of animals: the gristly and knobbly bits, encased in a tasteless, processed

shell that coats your mouth in fat. But a pie is only as good as the quality of its ingredients, and happily there now seems to be a pie renaissance underway with lots of new companies producing fabulous pies, baking only the best fillings under the lid.

Pies are great for entertaining, as they can be prepared days in advance and make a fabulous centrepiece. They are also a great way of using up leftovers, transforming them from yesterday's roast into steaming loveliness. And they freeze well too. Regardless of calorie count, I cannot think of anything so wholesome and nurturing for children, so comforting as a treat or so perfect for a big occasion as a well-made pie.

Pies are very social dishes and for this reason I have included numerous recipes written by family and friends. They are all about sharing and as such encapsulate some of the greatest joys in life. A pie makes an excellent gift. You will be very popular with friends if you bring one along when staying for the weekend (one less meal for your host to cook). During the days and nights of writing this book I have cooked hundreds of pies, baking on average about three different flavours a day. My kitchen has been groaning with pies and being the offspring of two war babies I loathe waste, so every visitor or person I have visited has had at least one pie pressed upon them. I can often been found with a pie in the bottom of my handbag, just in case I see a hungry-looking friend. They have always been delighted to receive it.

I hope you enjoy cooking from this book, getting it dirty, splattering it with ingredients. I hope you enjoy the smells, the sound of gentle bubbling, the peace of mixing and rolling the pastry, the excitement of fetching a pie from the oven. But most of all I hope you enjoy sharing the results of your labours with those that you love.

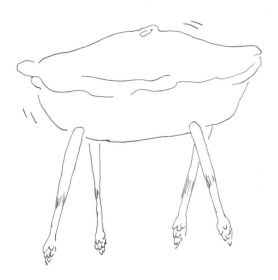

MAKING PASTRY

Pastry is as easy as pie. It really is a doddle. It's just a simple mixture of flour, fat and liquid to bind.

Use a nice fine flour; the best you can lay your mitts on. I like to use natural fats in my pastry, avoiding anything containing hydrogenated vegetable fats such as margarine and some shortenings. Admittedly, these do make pastry easier to work with, as they melt at a higher temperature and don't become as oily, but they're difficult to digest and I personally think they taste foul. Butter and suet, on the other hand, are whole foods. The body recognises them and can digest them easily. I use butter for shortcrust pastry, which makes a wonderful, light, biscuit-like pastry. Suet makes a pastry that's really easy to handle. I've found it holds its shape best too as it does not shrink or crumble. If you're a novice, try a suet crust as it is pretty foolproof.

Pastry is usually made up of approximately two-thirds flour, one-third fat and enough liquid to bind it. The quantities you will need may vary as may the type of flour, fat or liquid used. Have a play. You can also add any flavour you like: spices, cheese, herbs, horseradish, mustard (English mustard powder is great mixed into a cheesy pastry; grainy mustard adds a great texture), and even vegetables or bacon can be added to savoury pastry, just like bread. For sweet pastries, try sugar, honey, spices like vanilla, cinnamon or nutmeg, rosewater, dried fruit or herbs such as lavender and even crystallised petals. Let your imagination be your guide, but make sure what you add complements the filling and enhances the flavour. When adding an extra ingredient, be mindful of the consistency of the pastry – some ingredients can dry it out, while others make it too sticky. This can be fixed by adding either a little flour or a little liquid.

Stay chilled

Keeping everything as cold as possible (including bowls, hands and ingredients) makes for the best pastry. That said, I have a warm kitchen and warm hands, supposedly two of pastry's biggest enemies, but I still manage to make perfectly decent pastry. Some people suggest putting everything in the fridge for an hour before starting. If the fat becomes too warm it will melt and be absorbed into the flour too much, which prevents the flour from absorbing enough water, and the result is pastry that's too crumbly and difficult to roll. This is particularly the case if you are working with a pastry with a high fat content, like puff pastry.

If the pastry is greasy and heavy once cooked, you will have overworked it, or it got too hot before cooking and the fat melted. Body heat and overworking can cause the fat to melt, so keep cool and handle it as little as possible. One way to avoid this problem is to mix the pastry in a food processor, which is also super speedy. I still love making pastry by hand, though; rubbing the butter into the flour is really therapeutic. My daughter Coco loves measuring out ingredients and getting her little hands stuck into the flour.

Watch your liquid

The more liquid you add, the more the pastry shrinks when cooked. So, if you take it out of the oven and it's done just that and is also quite tough, you'll know how to solve it next time: just reduce the amount of liquid. On the other hand, pastry needs liquid to react with the flour to lengthen the gluten strands, so if you haven't added enough it will crack and crumble when you roll it.

Time to relax

For a similar reason, pastry is best made the day before and kept in the fridge. This gives the gluten strands in the flour time to relax; they become less elastic and the pastry will be easier to roll out. If your pastry shrinks but isn't tough, you probably didn't chill it enough.

Wrapped in cling film, pastry will keep happily enough in the fridge for up to three days, or in the freezer for up to three

months, ready for an emergency pie moment. Store it as a flatish disc, as this will make it easier to roll out when you want to use it. Pastry is easiest to work with at room temperature, so take it out of the fridge half an hour before you use it.

A note about "soggy bottoms"

Soggy bottoms are something I detest but, it seems, this is a matter of taste: soggy bottoms have their fans too. To avoid the dreaded soggy bottom of a tart or pie, the pastry case needs to be cooked (blind baked) before filling. To do this, line your pie dish or tart tin with pastry and prick the base a few times with a fork. If you have time, let him have a little rest in the fridge for about 10 minutes, as this reduces shrinkage of the pastry shell. Cover with greaseproof paper or foil and for puff pastries fill with a layer of dried beans, pulses or rice to stop the base from literally puffing up and making it impossible to fill. To crisp the base further, remove the foil and beans and pop it back in the oven for 5 minutes. If the edges look like they may burn, just cover with foil. Finish baking according to the recipe.

Soggy bottoms can also affect pie tops. A pie funnel will prevent this by supporting the pastry so it doesn't sag into the filling and boil rather than bake. In addition, the funnel forms a vent through which the steam that builds up under the crust during cooking can escape (this also helps to stop the filling boiling over the edges). To use a pie funnel, place it in the centre of the pie dish before spooning in the filling mixture around it. Cover with pastry in the normal way, making a hole with a knife through the pastry into the top of the funnel.

Funnels are not absolutely essential, however, and you can achieve much the same result simply by ensuring the pie dish is the correct size for the amount of filling. Pile the filling full to keep the pastry elevated, then cut a small hole in the middle of the pastry to allow the steam out.

Choosing the right pie dish

Pie dishes come in all shapes and sizes, from wide shallow dishes to deep pudding basins. Where I've not given you a size, you can use any shape you like – all you need to do is use an ovenproof vessel of the right volume. You should allow approximately 350ml (12fl oz) per hungry adult.

Pie dishes often have the volume listed on the bottom, but if yours doesn't you can measure it using a measuring jug. Do this by pouring water from the jug into the dish and counting up, not the other way round! It's important to fill your pie dish to the top, so if needs be choose something a little too small rather than too big. If you have leftover filling, you can always freeze it and use it for your next pie.

Individual pie, dishes approx. 350ml (12fl oz) each
4 people, dish approx. 1.5 litres (2¾ pints)
6 people, dish approx. 2 litres (3½ pints)
8 people, dish approx. 2.8 litres (5 pints)

Less is more

Restrain yourself when it comes to decorating the top of your pie, as over-decorating can make the lid soggy because of the double thickness (keep an eye on your kids here, as they love the decorating bit and sometimes get carried away).

If this all sounds a little ominous and off-putting don't worry! These things are easy to get right with the tiniest amount of practice. Everyone should have their own way of making pastry; these are only my personal preferences. As my mother used to say, there's more than one way to skin a rabbit. Have I enthused you yet? I hope so. It's easy-peasy. Give it a go.

Shortcrust pastry

The recipe opposite gives the amount of butter, flour, salt and liquid and you'll need for making 300g (10oz) of pastry. It is best made the day before. First, cut the butter into cubes, then put it into a food processor with the flour and salt. Using the cutting blade, blitz until it resembles fine breadcrumbs. Add the chilled water or egg a little at a time. The amount of liquid you need will always be an approximation, as all flours are slightly different. If it is a very damp day, you will need even less liquid in the mixture. Pulse the mixture until it binds together into a ball. Scoop it out of the food processor and dust it with flour. Form the dough into a thick disc. Cover with cling film and chill for a minimum of 1 hour in the fridge. Allow the pastry to come back to room temperature before using a floured board to roll it out.

How thinly you roll out your pastry is a matter of preference, and will depend on your choice of pie dish and the type of pastry you're using. I tend to use a thickness of 3–5mm/⅛–¼in, so if you're starting out, I would go with this.

Sweet shortcrust pastry

For sweet shortcrust pastry, you'll need to reduce the amount of flour and, once you've whizzed the flour and butter to breadcrumbs, add 1 tablespoon of caster sugar. Then pulse until mixed. (See the panel on the right for the amounts required for making 300g /10oz.)

Vanilla pastry replace some of the water with ½ teaspoon of vanilla extract.

Rosewater pastry substitute a tablespoon of water with rosewater.

Cinnamon pastry add a teaspoon of ground cinnamon with the flour.

Filo and puff pastry

I should probably try to make filo pastry. Apparently it is an art form that takes generations of experience to perfect, so I stick to the shop-bought stuff as it's usually excellent.

Puff pastry is the other kind of pastry for which there's no shame in buying from the shops. Making from scratch requires so much rolling and refrigerating that it can seem far too time-consuming unless you are dedicated.

SHORTCRUST PASTRY MAKES 300G (10OZ)

100g (3½oz) unsalted butter, straight from the fridge

200g (7oz) plain flour, cold if possible

a pinch of salt

1–2 tbsp chilled water or 1 small beaten egg

SWEET SHORTCRUST PASTRY MAKES 300G (10OZ)

100g (3½oz) unsalted butter, straight from the fridge

150g (5oz) plain flour, cold if possible

1 tbsp caster sugar

1–2 tbsp chilled water or 1 small beaten egg

Baking on an Aga

I love my Aga. I love the way it gently breathes and warms the kitchen. Every pie in this book has been cooked on and in my Aga.

My basic method for cooking a pie involves first preparing the filling and then baking the filling in a pastry case or just covering with pastry. I tend to cook the filling on a simmering plate, using a large cast-iron or ceramic casserole. If it is cooking too fast, I put a coin under the pan. When it comes to baking, I usually pop the pie on the grid shelf on the lowest set of runners in the roasting oven, then check after about 15 minutes and cover with foil if it looks like the pastry is brown enough. Below is a general guide to converting the temperatures used in this book for your Aga.

Conventional oven	Fan oven	Fahrenheit	Gas Mark	AGA 2 oven	AGA 3 & 4 oven
150°C	130°C	300°F	2	Simmering oven	Simmering oven
170°C	150°C	325°F	3	Grid shelf on floor of roasting oven and cold plain shelf above	Grid shelf on floor of baking oven
180°C	160°C	350°F	4	Grid shelf on floor of roasting oven and cold plain shelf above	Lowest runner of baking oven
190°C	170°C	375°F	5	Grid shelf on floor of roasting oven	Top of baking oven
200°C	180°C	400°F	6	Lowest set of runners in roasting oven	
220°C	200°C	425°F	7	3rd or 4th set of runners in roasting oven	

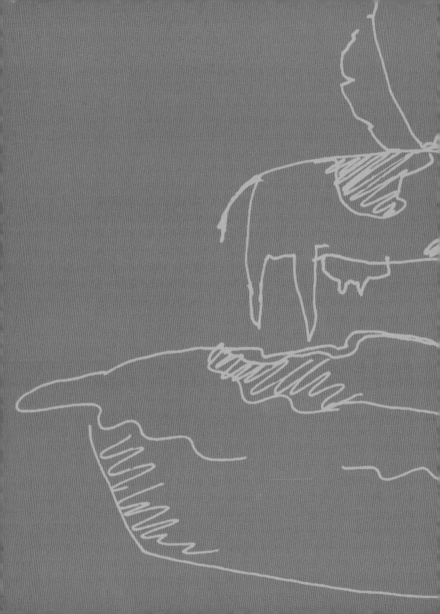

Beefy Pies

My son Felix loves this pie. It is super tasty with lots of lovely chunks of meat and thick gravy: a very traditional beef pie. Felix is a solid little carnivore!

BEEF WITH CARROTS

SERVES 6

1.2kg (2½lb) chuck stewing or braising steak, cut into 4cm (1½in) cubes

1½ tbsp plain flour, seasoned with salt and pepper

1 tbsp olive oil

25g (1oz) butter

18 pearl (or 'button') onions, peeled and trimmed

300ml (10fl oz) beef stock

1 tsp cayenne pepper or paprika

1 tsp dried thyme

1 handful fresh flat leaf parsley, chopped

1 bay leaf

450g (1lb) carrots, peeled and chopped

1 tbsp Worcestershire sauce

1 egg, beaten

400g (14oz) good-quality butter puff pastry

Roll the meat in the seasoned flour. Put the oil and butter into a large pan on a medium to high heat and fry the meat in batches, turning until browned all over but still pink in the middle. Don't put too much meat in the pan at any one time. Remove the meat and reserve for later.

In a pan, boil the onions in the stock for about 10 minutes until they are just tender. Strain, keeping the liquid, and put the onions to one side. Return the meat to the large pan with the cooking liquid from the onions, add the cayenne to the meat and stir through (you can use paprika instead of cayenne pepper for a milder dish). Add the herbs and bring to the boil. Reduce the heat, cover the pan and simmer for 1 hour. Check and stir occasionally, adding a dash of stock if more liquid is needed.

After an hour, stir in the carrots, the cooked onions and the Worcestershire sauce. Simmer gently for a further 30 minutes until the meat and the carrots are tender. Preheat the oven to 220°C (425°F/Gas 7). Spoon the stew into a pie dish and brush the rim of the dish with a little of the beaten egg.

Roll out the puff pastry so it is big enough to cover the pie dish. Place the rolled pastry over the top of the dish, trimming the edges to fit. Press the edges down with your thumb and decorate the pie with shapes cut from the excess pastry. Cut a small hole in the top to let the steam escape and brush the pastry all over with the beaten egg. Place in the oven and bake for 20 minutes.

I like to serve this pie with boiled new potatoes and runner beans.

Making this pie is a joy, as the smell of the Moroccan spices fills the house. If you like a bit of heat, add a teaspoon of harissa with the spices. It is also fabulous served with saffron mash (see page 124).

BEEF WITH BLACK OLIVES

SERVES 6

FOR THE FILLING:

2 tbsp olive oil

500g (1lb) chuck stewing or braising steak, cut into 4cm (1½in) cubes

1 tbsp plain flour, seasoned with salt and pepper

a knob of butter

3 onions, sliced

6 cloves garlic, chopped

1 handful fresh flat leaf parsley, chopped

1 tsp ground cumin

1 tsp ground coriander

1 tsp ground ginger

1 cinnamon stick

400g (14oz) tin plum tomatoes

150g (5oz) black olives, pitted

150ml (5fl oz) water

1 tbsp tomato purée

salt and freshly ground black pepper

ingredients continued

First make the filling. Heat the oil in a large casserole on a high heat. Coat the meat in the seasoned flour and fry until browned all over. Remove the meat from the pan and set aside.

Reduce the heat and add the butter to the pan. Stir in the onions and gently stew for 10 minutes or until translucent. Keep checking and stirring to make sure the onions do not burn. Throw in the garlic, parsley and spices, and stir for a couple of minutes. Return the meat to the pan, then pour in the tomatoes, olives and water. Stir through the tomato purée. Mash up the tomatoes a bit with your spoon and scrape the bottom of the pan to keep it from sticking. Gently simmer for 2 hours – keep checking to make sure it does not burn or stick to the bottom of the pan and give it a gentle stir; add some more water if it starts to dry out.

While the filling is simmering, prepare the pastry. Mix all the dry ingredients together in a large bowl. Rub in the butter between your thumb and fingers until it looks like breadcrumbs. Add the milk a little at a time and combine until you have a soft dough. Depending on the type of flour you are using, you may need a little more or less milk than suggested. Roll the dough into a ball, cover it in cling film and pop it in the fridge until needed.

recipe continued

Beef with Black Olives (continued)

FOR THE PASTRY:

250g (9oz) self-raising flour

1 tsp baking powder

½ tsp bicarbonate of soda

½ tsp salt

2 tsp ground turmeric

100g (3½oz) butter, cubed

100ml (3½fl oz) milk

Preheat the oven to 220°C (425°F/Gas 7). Once the filling has finished simmering and is an aromatic tender stew with a nice thick rich sauce, remove the cinnamon stick. Taste the filling and season it with salt and pepper accordingly. Pour the mixture into a medium pie dish.

Roll out the pastry to make a lid for the dish. Brush the edges of the dish with water so the lid will stick. Cover the dish with the pastry, press down the edges and trim. Cut a small hole in the top to let the steam escape, and bake the pie for 20 minutes.

I like to serve this pie with boiled sweet potatoes, tossed in butter and chopped fresh parsley.

Robert is the brilliant development chef I work with on my pie range. This is his fabulous rework of the Great British Sunday lunch.

BEEF, ALE & MUSHROOM PIE WITH YORKSHIRE PUDDING LID

by Robert Barker

SERVES 4

FOR THE FILLING:

600g (1lb 5oz) chuck stewing or braising steak, cut into 3cm (1in) cubes

1 bouquet garni

1 small bottle 'real' ale (about 300ml/10fl oz)

2 tbsp olive oil

1 large onion, diced

1 clove garlic, diced

2 carrots, peeled and diced

1 stick celery, diced

1 tbsp plain flour

150ml (5fl oz) beef stock or just enough to cover the meat

150g (5oz) field mushrooms, sliced

1 handful fresh flat leaf parsley, chopped

salt and freshly ground black pepper

ingredients continued

Place the cubed beef and bouquet garni in a large bowl and pour over the ale. Cover with cling film and refrigerate overnight. The next day, strain and dry the beef, reserving the ale and bouquet garni until needed.

Heat the oil over a high heat in a large pan. Quickly fry the beef in batches until browned all over, then set aside. Reduce the heat and gently fry the onion, garlic, carrots and celery for about 10 minutes. Stir in the flour, and continue frying and stirring for a further 5 minutes, making sure there are no lumps of flour.

Add the reserved ale and bouquet garni to the pan and simmer until the liquid is reduced by half. Then add the stock, browned meat and mushrooms to the pot. Simmer gently for 1½ hours, stirring occasionally to make sure the mixture is not burning or sticking to the pan. Discard the bouquet garni, then stir in the parsley and season to taste.

Meanwhile, make the Yorkshire pudding batter. Put the flour and salt in a large bowl, then whisk in the eggs one at a time. Add the milk, and whisk until you have a smooth batter. Strain the mixture through a sieve and chill for 1 hour.

recipe continued

Beef, Ale & Mushroom Pie
with Yorkshire Pudding Lid (continued)

FOR THE YORKSHIRE PUDDING LID:

150g (5oz) plain flour

1 tsp salt

2 eggs

300ml (10fl oz) milk

15g (½oz) lard

Preheat the oven to 220°C (425°F/Gas 7). To cook the Yorkshire pudding lid, heat the lard in the oven for 5 minutes in a tin the same size and shape as the top of the pie dish. Carefully pour the batter into the hot fat and cook in the oven for 30 minutes until risen and golden brown.

When ready to serve, simply pour the meat into a pie dish and top with the Yorkshire pudding lid before taking it to the table.

Serve with roast potatoes, Brussels sprouts and carrots.

Osso Bucco is one of my son Felix's favourite
dishes; one he likes me to make on his birthday!

OSSO BUCCO PIE

SERVES 4

FOR THE FILLING:

2 tbsp olive oil

4 large slices of beef shin
or osso bucco with bones,
approx. 2kg (4lb 8oz) in
total (see tip, page 37)

1 tbsp plain flour, seasoned
with salt and pepper

a knob of butter

1 large red onion, chopped

2 carrots, peeled and
chopped

1 stick celery, chopped

2 cloves garlic, chopped

salt and freshly ground
black pepper

1 small glass white wine
(about 150ml / 5fl oz)

400g (14oz) tin plum
tomatoes

1 small wine glass beef stock
(about 150ml / 5fl oz)

Heat the oil in a casserole big enough to take the meat all in one
layer. Coat the osso bucco in the seasoned flour and fry over a
medium-high heat, turning once, until lightly browned on both sides.
Remove from the pan and set aside.

Reduce the heat, add the butter and gently fry the onion, carrots and
celery for 10 minutes. Mix through the garlic and season. Fry for a
couple more minutes and then pour in the wine. Scrape the bottom
of the pan with a wooden spoon to dislodge any flour sticking to
the bottom. Simmer for 5 minutes. Throw in the tomatoes, stock and
orange peel, giving the tomatoes a bit of a mash with your spoon.
Return the meat to the pan, submerging it in the sauce. Leave the pot
to simmer gently for 1½ hours, stirring from time to time. Add some
water if it starts to dry out.

Preheat the oven to 220°C (425°F/Gas 7). Meanwhile, make the
pastry by mixing all the dry ingredients together in a large bowl,
using your hands to mix in the water until you have a soft dough.
Knead for a couple of minutes until it becomes smooth and elastic.
Cover with cling film and set aside.

2 strips orange peel cut with
  a potato peeler
1 handful fresh flat leaf
  parsley, chopped
1 egg, beaten

FOR THE PASTRY:
100g (3½oz) prepared suet,
  such as Atora
200g (7oz) self-raising flour
a large pinch of salt
4 tbsp very cold water

When your meat is extremely tender and beginning to fall off the bone, lift it out of the sauce and put to one side to cool. Simmer the sauce for a further 15 minutes to thicken. Once the meat has cooled, cut it into large chunks and throw out any globby bits you don't like the look of. Scoop the marrow from the centre of the bones and add to the sauce. Take the sauce off the heat and throw away the orange peel. Stir in the meat and parsley, taste and season again if necessary.

Fill an ovenproof dish with the mixture. Roll out the pastry so it is large enough to cover the pie. Brush the edges of the dish with a little of the beaten egg and cover with the pastry lid. Brush all over the top of the pastry with the egg, then press the edge of the pastry down with your thumb or the tines of a fork. Trim any excess pastry hanging over the edge using a sharp knife. Cut two holes in the top to let the steam escape, place in the oven and bake for 20 minutes.

I like to serve this pie with fried baby courgettes, or with young beetroot leaves.

This is a traditional British dish. My parents used to serve it at dinner parties and I thought it was very chic.

BEEF WELLINGTON

SERVES 6

1kg (2lb 4oz) beef fillet in one piece

salt and freshly ground black pepper

1 tbsp olive oil

100g (3½oz) butter

1 onion, finely chopped

250g (9oz) field mushrooms, finely chopped

3 cloves garlic, finely chopped

1 handful fresh flat leaf parsley, chopped and stalks removed

2 tbsp brandy

2 tbsp double cream

375g (13oz) good-quality butter puff pastry

1 egg, beaten

Season the beef with salt and pepper. Heat the oil in a large pan over a high heat. As soon as it is hot, quickly fry the meat until browned all over. Remove the meat from the pan and set it aside on a plate. If you like rare meat, this is perfect; if you prefer it more cooked or it is a thick piece, then brown for longer.

Reduce the heat, add the butter to the pan and gently fry the onion for about 15 minutes or until soft. Add the mushrooms and garlic, and cook for a further 15 minutes, stirring from time to time. Stir through the parsley, and then pour in the brandy. Simmer for 5 minutes, then add the cream and stir it through. Remove the pan from the heat and allow the contents to cool. Meanwhile, preheat the oven to 220°C (425°F/Gas 7).

Roll out the pastry into a large sheet that is large enough to wrap the meat in. Spread the cooled mushroom mixture in a layer over the pastry, leaving about 3cm (1in) around the edge. Brush the edge with a little of the beaten egg. Place the meat in the middle and carefully bring together the two long sides of pastry up and over the fillet. Gently pinch the sides together and then roll to make a neat seam at the top. Tuck the pastry flaps under at each end and gently set it in a roasting tin.

Brush all over the top of the pastry with a little more of the beaten egg and allow to dry for 10 minutes. Then brush over with egg once more. This gives the pastry shell a bit more strength and will help to stop it falling apart when sliced. Place it in the oven and roast for 20 minutes. Once cooked, remove from the oven and allow to stand for 10 minutes before carving.

I love this pie; it is a proper beef pie with gorgeous gravy and masses of flavour, guaranteed to satisfy. I like to serve it with mash and buttered Savoy cabbage.

BEEF WITH BUTTON MUSHROOMS & RED WINE

SERVES 6

1.5kg (3lb 5oz) chuck stewing or braising steak, cut into 4cm (1½in) cubes

30g (1¼oz) plain flour, seasoned with salt and pepper

4 tbsp olive oil

115g (4oz) pancetta, cut into little sticks

½ bottle full-bodied red wine, Merlot or Burgundy

300ml (10fl oz) beef stock

1 bouquet garni

salt and freshly ground black pepper

20 pearl (or 'button') onions, peeled and trimmed

225g (8oz) button mushrooms

30g (1¼oz) butter

salt and freshly ground black pepper

1 egg, beaten

450g (1lb) good-quality butter puff pastry

Coat the beef cubes thoroughly with the seasoned flour. Heat half the olive oil in a large saucepan on a high heat – use an ovenproof saucepan with a tight-fitting lid. Fry the pancetta in the oil until browned and remove it from the pan, then add the meat and fry in batches until browned all over, adding a little more oil if necessary. Set the meat aside with the pancetta.

Reduce the heat to medium, pour in half the wine and bring to the boil, using a wooden spoon to scrape up the gubbins that have stuck to the bottom. Return the meat and pancetta to the pot. Pour in the rest of the wine and just enough of the stock to leave the top halves of the uppermost pieces of meat showing above the liquid. Add the bouquet garni, stir and season with pepper. Pop the lid on the saucepan and simmer in the oven for 1½ hours.

Meanwhile, simmer the onions in a small pan in the remaining stock for 5 minutes. Remove the onions and discard the stock. Fry the onions and mushrooms gently in the rest of the oil and the butter for 10 minutes, and then set aside until needed. Preheat the oven to 220°C (425°F/Gas 7). Once the meat has finished simmering, remove the bouquet garni and stir the onions and mushrooms through. Taste for seasoning.

Spoon the mixture into a pie dish, ensuring the meat is piled high in the centre to support the pastry. Brush the rim of the pie dish with a little of the beaten egg. Roll out the pastry and cover the pie. Trim the pastry around the edge, and press to seal with a fork around the rim. Cut a hole in the top to let the steam escape and brush the pastry all over with beaten egg. Bake the pie in the oven for 30 minutes.

Deliciously sweet with a gorgeous rich colour. Adding the sweet potato to the mash makes a nice alternative to just potatoes and is also lovely with bangers. Don't worry about the alcohol in the lager; it burns off in the cooking.

BEEF & BEER PIE WITH SWEET POTATO MASH

SERVES 6

FOR THE FILLING:

1kg (2lb 4oz) chuck stewing or braising steak, cut into 4cm (1½in) cubes

1 tbsp plain flour, seasoned with salt and pepper

4 tbsp olive oil

2 knobs of butter

2 large red onions, chopped

6 large carrots, peeled and chopped into 1cm (½in) cubes

300ml (10fl oz) lager

6 juniper berries, crushed

2 sprigs rosemary

2 sprigs thyme

2 tbsp Worcestershire sauce

2 tbsp soft light brown sugar

300ml (10fl oz) beef stock

ingredients continued

Roll the meat in the seasoned flour. Put the oil into a large pan on a medium to high heat and fry the meat in batches until browned all over. Don't put too much meat in the pan at any one time or it won't brown properly. Remove the meat from the pan and reserve for later.

Reduce the heat to medium, add the butter, then gently fry the onions and carrots until the onions are soft – about 10 minutes. Return the meat to the pan and add the lager, juniper berries, rosemary, thyme, Worcestershire sauce, brown sugar and beef stock. Gently simmer for 1½ hours, stirring from time to time, and adding more stock if necessary.

Meanwhile, make the mash. Boil all the potatoes in plenty of salted water until they are very soft when poked with a sharp knife. Drain the potatoes well and then mash with the butter and plenty of salt and pepper. I use a mouli (pictured on page 105) for a lovely lump-free mash. Set aside.

recipe continued

1 handful fresh flat leaf
  parsley, chopped

salt and freshly ground
  black pepper

FOR THE MASH:

4 small Maris Piper
  potatoes, peeled
  and cubed

2 small sweet potatoes,
  peeled and cubed

50g (2oz) butter

Preheat the oven to 220°C (425°F/Gas 7). Once the meat is done, remove the herb stalks and stir through the chopped parsley. Taste and season with salt and pepper accordingly. Pour the mixture into your pie dish and top with the mash by spooning large dollops all over, then using the back of your spoon to smooth over until the meat is completely covered. Take a fork and rough the surface of the mash into small peaks, which will become lovely and brown with crispy bits. Bake uncovered for 25 minutes or until piping hot in the middle and golden on top.

Serve with buttered runner beans.

This pie is served at my brother Tom's fantastic pub. While I was living in Australia he called me up and in a very excited voice said, "Soph, I've bought a pub and named it after you." "Thanks, that's so sweet of you," I replied. He giggled, "Yes. It's called The Cow."

COW PIE *by William Leigh*

SERVES 6

4 slices of beef shin about 2.5cm (1in) thick (see tip opposite)

about 2 tbsp vegetable oil

sea salt and a fully charged pepper mill

4½ or 5 large onions, finely sliced into half moons (you want more than you think)

2–3 cloves garlic, finely sliced

2 handfuls button mushrooms, halved and quartered, or 12 shucked oysters (see tip opposite)

1 monstrous bunch of fresh herbs, including thyme, bay leaves, rosemary, sage, parsley stalks and tarragon (only a touch of rosemary and sage as they are so vicious)

375g (13oz) good-quality butter puff pastry for 1 large pie, or 500g (1lb) for 6 individual pies

1 egg yolk, beaten with 1 tbsp milk

This recipe is a corruption of the mighty "Grillade des marinieres du Rhône" as taught to me by the highly estimable chef Jeremy Lee.

So, to begin with, pop a large pan on the stove over a high heat. It should be big enough to hold all the beef in one layer. Now turn to the beef; rub this lightly with oil and season well with salt and coarsely milled pepper. By this time your pan should be good and hot. Bung in a good glug (more than you expect) of the oil. Don't worry; we'll be dumping it later. Then chuck in your beef in one nice even layer. Leave it! Don't do any cheffy jiggling of the pan and don't do the housewife "I'll just take a peek". Just let it colour for a goodly long time. But don't by any stretch of the imagination burn it! It should be a good mahogany colour and a little crisp when you eventually flip it. Then repeat on the other side – you won't be able to get such a good colour or "maillard reaction" on the second side. Then remove the beef and tip away any excess oil, but not quite all. You still need a touch in the pan to cook the rest of the ingredients in.

Return the pan to the stove, turn the heat down, then dump in the onions and garlic and season timidly. Allow these to soften ever so slightly for about a minute or two and then add your other ingredients, either mushrooms or oysters, followed swiftly by the beef and the mammoth faggot of herbs. Turn this all around in the pan so the beef is nestled lovingly in mounds of onions. Cover the pot with a tight-fitting lid or, better still, foil and a lid. Leave on the lowest possible heat for 3 to 4 hours. I normally use the smallest burner on the stove on the lowest setting, with a heat diffuser or tray under the pan. Don't worry about adding any liquid. That's the joy of this dish: the beef cooks in the juice from the onions and vice versa. If you add too much liquid, the onions have a tendency to boil and never fully descend to the great rich sludginess you want from them.

Now, when the beef is completely cooked through and just falling off the bone and the onions have melted through, leaving a beautiful golden swamp of juice, it is ready to take off the heat. Leave it to cool for an hour or so before attempting to break it up, otherwise you will just end up with white-hot onions dripping down your arm and a mess in the pot. Not fun, believe me! When the beef has cooled slightly, and therefore firmed up a little, break it away from the bone into forkful-sized chunks. Remove any of the skin and discard. Poke out the marrow from the middle of the bone into the onions. Now remove the bouquet garni from the onions and pop the beef back in. Taste it for seasoning and adjust as necessary.

The pie filling is now ready. Preheat the oven to 180°–200°C (350°–400°F/Gas 4–6). All you need to do is bang it in a suitable pie dish, either one big one or if you are feeling terribly posh have individual ones. Cover with good puff pastry, egg wash it with a bit of beaten yolk and milk and bang it in a goodly hot oven till puffed and golden.

Serve at once with mashed potatoes, or chips if the beery night seems somewhat more appropriate!

Tips – Getting the beef shin: You will need to acquire four slices of beef shin, about 2.5cm (1in) thick and cut right through the bone. In Italian they call this "osso bucco", meaning literally "on the bone". Your butcher should be able to do this, but may need a bit of notice. The rest of the ingredients should be far simpler to lay your hands on.

Using oysters: If you want to make an oyster pie, substitute about 12 rock oysters for the mushrooms. I like to buy the Pacific oysters from Falmouth Bay. Shuck them with an oyster knife, reserving any juice and removing any little bits of shell you find. Pass the juice through a sieve and pop the oysters back into it. Use both the oysters and their juice in the pie.

I have only recently started to make lasagne, having been put off by years of school lasagne. But now I like to think of it as a pie made with pasta layers rather than pastry. This is my version. I am sure it is totally wonky, but it tastes great and my kids love it.

LASAGNE

SERVES 4 HUNGRY ADULTS OR 8 TINY CHILDREN

3 tbsp olive oil

a knob of butter

1 red onion, chopped

1 stick celery, chopped

2 carrots, peeled and chopped

½ tsp dried thyme

salt and freshly ground black pepper

3 cloves garlic, chopped

150g (5oz) chestnut mushrooms, chopped

500g (1lb) beef mince

400g (14oz) tin plum tomatoes

2 tbsp Worcestershire sauce

1 tbsp tomato purée

400ml (14oz) beef stock

1 handful fresh flat leaf parsley, chopped

ingredients continued

Heat the oil and butter in a large pot over a medium heat. Add the onion, celery, carrots and thyme and fry gently. Grind in plenty of black pepper. Allow everything to gently sizzle away for 10 minutes, giving it the occasional stir. Add the garlic and mushrooms and continue cooking for a further 10 minutes.

Stir in the mince with a wooden spoon, breaking it up into largish chunks. Fry it until it has browned and any liquid in the pot has evaporated. Drop in the tomatoes, and add the Worcestershire sauce, tomato purée and beef stock, stirring them through. Leave it to simmer gently for 1 hour, checking from time to time to make sure it hasn't dried out or stuck to the pot, adding more liquid if necessary. Taste and season accordingly. Once the meat mixture has simmered for an hour, remove from the heat and stir in the parsley.

Meanwhile, make the béchamel sauce. Melt the butter in a large pan, stir in the flour and allow it to bubble for a couple of minutes without burning. Pour in all of the milk, add the bay leaf and nutmeg and vigorously whisk the mixture until it is smooth. Let it gently bubble away for 10 minutes, whisking occasionally. Then set it aside until it is needed. Just before using, remove the bay leaf and add three-quarters of the Parmesan and a little extra milk if needed, heating it through gently.

recipe continued

Lasagne (CONTINUED)

8 lasagne sheets, approx.,
  cooked as directed on the
  packet (see tip)

FOR THE BÉCHAMEL:

50g (2oz) butter

2 tbsp plain flour

800ml (1½ pints) milk,
  plus a little extra

1 bay leaf

¼ tsp ground nutmeg

75g (2¾oz) Parmesan,
  grated

Preheat the oven to 200°C (400°F/Gas 6). To assemble the lasagne, spoon a layer of the meat into a large ovenproof dish, cover with a layer of béchamel and then a layer of cooked lasagne sheets. Repeat this process, finishing with a layer of béchamel. Sprinkle the rest of the grated Parmesan on top. Place in the oven and bake for 30 minutes.

I like to serve lasagne with a fresh green salad with lots of herbs, and garlic bread.

Tip: The exact number of lasagne sheets you use will depend on the size of your dish and how big the sheets are.

My wonderful brother Jasper suggested adding horseradish to this pie and indeed it is excellent. It is named in his honour.

Jasper's Steak & Kidney Pie

SERVES 4

1 tbsp olive oil

a knob of butter

250g (9oz) chestnut mushrooms, sliced

500g (1lb) chuck stewing or braising steak, cut into 4cm (1½in) cubes

300g (10oz) pork kidneys, trimmed and cut into 4cm (1½in) cubes

1 tbsp plain flour, seasoned with salt and pepper

300ml (10fl oz) beef stock

18 pearl (or 'button') onions, peeled and trimmed

1 small glass red wine (about 150ml / 5fl oz)

1 tbsp horseradish, either sauce or freshly grated

3 splashes of Worcestershire sauce

salt and freshly ground black pepper

1 egg, beaten

300g (10oz) good-quality butter puff pastry

Heat half the oil and the butter in a large pan over a medium heat. Drop in the mushrooms and sauté for 10 minutes or until cooked through. Remove them from the pot and set them aside.

Add the rest of the oil to the pan and increase the heat to high. Coat the steak and kidneys with the seasoned flour. Fry the steak and kidneys in batches until they have all browned slightly, then remove from the pan and set aside with the mushrooms.

Pour the beef stock into a small pan, plop in the onions and boil for 10 minutes. Meanwhile, turn the heat under the large pan back down to medium and add the wine, horseradish and Worcestershire sauce, scraping up any flour that has stuck to the bottom. Let it bubble until you have a thickish sauce.

Add the browned meat, mushrooms, onions and beef stock to the sauce and simmer gently for 1½ hours. Keep an eye on it and stir occasionally, adding some water if it looks like it is drying out; the mixture should be quite sloppy. Season.

Preheat the oven to 220°C (425°F/Gas 7). Pour the steak and kidney mixture into a pie dish, making sure that it is pretty full, otherwise it will boil and fail to turn crisp. Brush some of the beaten egg around the rim of the pie dish.

Roll out the pastry, cover the pie, trim around the edge and press it down around the rim with your thumb to seal. Decorate the top with shapes cut from the pastry trimmings. Cut a small hole in the top to let the steam escape and brush the top with the beaten egg.

Cover with foil and place in the oven for 15 minutes. Remove the foil and cook for a further 15 minutes. Serve with roasted vegetables and mustard.

My mum's steak and kidney pudding is like her.
It's the best. This is her delicious recipe.

MY MUM'S STEAK & KIDNEY PUDDING *by Caroline Conran*

SERVES 6

You will need a 1-litre
(1¾-pint) pudding basin

FOR THE SUET PASTRY:

100g (3½oz) prepared
suet, such as Atora

225g (8oz) self-raising
flour

a large pinch of salt

iced water

FOR THE FILLING:

900g (2lb) chuck stewing
or braising steak, cut into
3cm (1in) cubes

225g (8oz) beef kidneys,
trimmed well and cut into
3cm (1in) cubes

3 tbsp plain flour, seasoned
with salt and pepper

50g (2oz) button mushrooms

1 tbsp Worcestershire sauce

a dash of Tabasco sauce

ingredients continued

First prepare the pastry. Mix the suet, flour and salt in a bowl and, using a tablespoon at a time, slowly add enough iced water to bind. This can be done in a food processor, but don't over-process the mixture. Cover the pastry with cling film and chill for 20 minutes. Keep about a quarter of the pastry back to make the lid, then roll out the other three-quarters to a thickness of about 3mm / ⅛in.

Butter the pudding basin. Line it with the rolled-out pastry, leaving about 3cm (1in) of pastry hanging over the top. Set aside.

Now make the filling by rolling the beef and kidney in the seasoned flour. Mix the meat with the mushrooms and pile it all into the pastry-lined basin. Sprinkle with the Worcestershire, Tabasco and oyster sauces. Pour in enough beef stock or water to fill two-thirds (or slightly more) of the dish. Season the filling with plenty of pepper.

Roll out the remaining pastry to make a lid. Cover the filling and fold the edges together to form a seal, pressing the edges of the pastry together lightly.

Cut a piece of foil large enough to cover the top of the pudding loosely: the pudding must have room to expand. Hold the foil in place by tying some string around it, just under the rim of the pudding basin. Make a handle by passing the string across the top loosely, two or three times and threading it under the rim-string (see pictured on page 44). Fasten it tightly at one side. Set the sealed pudding aside.

recipe continued

My Mum's Steak & Kidney Pudding (continued)

1 tbsp Chinese oyster sauce
a little beef stock (cube is okay) or water
freshly ground black pepper

Fill a large pan with a tightly fitting lid with enough water to come two-thirds of the way up the pudding basin. Bring the water to the boil and lower the pudding into the pan. Cover the large pan with a lid. (The first time I made the pudding I did not remember the lid or even dream that it was essential, silly idiot. After 4 hours the pudding was still more or less raw.) Add more boiling water as it evaporates and boils away and don't worry if the pudding leaks a bit. Continue topping up the boiling water as necessary for 4 to 5 hours.

Lift the pudding out of the pan and remove the foil. Wrap the basin in a white cloth or napkin with the top crust showing, browned and slightly fluffy, over the top of its white linen collar. If the crust has come in contact with the water it will be pale and glistening but still excellent to eat. Serve the fragrant pudding with a big spoon.

Accompany with small plainly boiled potatoes and carrots or any vegetable mash, and, if you like it, English mustard. I also like this with cabbage or purple sprouting broccoli.

More
Meaty Pies

This is a pie for hungry folk. It is very meaty with a great tang from the plums. Decorate the top with pastry flowers and leaves for a spectacular feast.

VENISON WITH PORT & PLUMS

SERVES 8

1kg (2lb 4oz) venison shoulder, leg or neck, cut into 4cm (2½in) cubes

FOR THE MARINADE:

½ bottle port

8 juniper berries, crushed

2 bay leaves, crumbled

4 cloves garlic, crushed

½ red onion, sliced

2 tbsp olive oil

salt and freshly ground black pepper

FOR THE FILLING:

2 tbsp olive oil

1 tbsp plain flour

150g (5oz) bacon lardons

1½ red onions, chopped

1 cinnamon stick

5 large unripe (so they are sour) red plums, halved and stoned

ingredients continued

Mix the meat with all the marinade ingredients in an airtight container. Leave to infuse for 4 hours or overnight in the fridge. Strain off the marinade and reserve, but throw out the onion and bay leaves.

Now make the filling by heating the oil in a large casserole over a medium to high heat. Coat the meat in the flour and fry it in batches until it has just browned on the outside. Once browned, put the meat to one side. Fry the bacon in the same casserole until it starts to brown, then reduce the heat. Add the onions and continue to fry for 10 minutes or until the onions are soft. Don't forget to stir them now and again, so they don't burn or get stuck to the pan.

Pour the marinade into the casserole and mix it in thoroughly, scraping up all the gubbins stuck to the bottom of the pan. Allow it to bubble away for about 5 minutes until it thickens. Throw in the meat, any juice and the cinnamon stick. Simmer gently for 1½ hours. Stir in the plums and allow to cool while you make the pastry.

Preheat the oven to 220°C (425°F/Gas 7). Make the pastry by mixing the suet, flour, white wine and salt together in a large bowl until you have a soft dough. Add a little more flour if it is sticky or water if it is too dry. Knead the dough for a couple of minutes until

recipe continued

FOR THE PASTRY:

100g (3½oz) prepared suet, such as Atora

200g (7oz) self-raising flour

4 tbsp white wine

a large pinch of salt

1 egg, beaten

it becomes smooth and a little elastic and then set it aside.

Spoon the venison mixture into a pie dish. Roll out the pastry to a size large enough to cover the pie dish. Brush the edges of the pie dish with a little of the beaten egg and cover with the pastry. Trim the edges, putting aside any excess pastry. Press down all around the rim with a fork. Cut shapes out of the extra pastry to decorate the top of the pie, cut a small hole in the top of the pie to let the steam escape and brush it again with beaten egg. Place it in the oven and bake for 25 minutes.

I like to serve this pie with pommes dauphinoise, carrots and Savoy cabbage.

Beautifully spicy and with a wonderful sweetness from the apricots, the herbs in this recipe add a lovely freshness.

MOROCCAN LAMB WITH APRICOTS

SERVES 4

FOR THE MARINADE:

3 tbsp harissa

2 tbsp olive oil

3 tbsp fresh lemon juice

3 cloves garlic, chopped

10g (¼oz) cinnamon sticks

2 tsp sesame seeds

1 tsp ground cumin

FOR THE FILLING:

550g (1lb 4oz) lamb, either leg or shoulder, cut into 4cm (1½in) cubes

1 tbsp olive oil

1 large onion, sliced

250g (9oz) dried apricots

1 tsp fresh thyme leaves

500ml (18fl oz) vegetable stock

ingredients continued

In a large ceramic bowl, combine all the marinade ingredients. Add the lamb, making sure it is well coated. Cover and leave for at least 1 hour or overnight in the fridge. Remove the meat from the marinade, keeping the marinade for later.

Preheat the oven to 150°C (300°F/Gas 2). Pour the oil into a large casserole over a high heat. Add the marinated lamb to the casserole in batches, fry quickly until browned, then set aside. Turn the heat down to medium. Add the onion and fry gently for 10 minutes.

Return the meat to the pan with any remaining marinade. Add the apricots, thyme and stock. Season the mixture well with salt and freshly ground black pepper. Bring to a simmer and then place it in the oven with the lid on. After one hour, remove from the oven and stir the mixture well. Turn the oven up to 220°C (425°F/Gas 7) and return the casserole, uncovered, to the oven for 1½ hours.

Remove the casserole from the oven, pick out the cinnamon sticks and discard. Allow the mixture to cool slightly before stirring in the herbs. Place the mixture in a pie dish and set aside.

recipe continued

salt and freshly ground
  black pepper

1 handful fresh coriander
  leaves, chopped

1 handful fresh mint leaves,
  chopped

FOR THE TOP:

300g (10oz) cumin
  puff pastry (see tip)

1 egg, beaten

Roll out the pastry large enough to cover the pie dish. Brush the rim of the pie dish with a little of the beaten egg. Cover the pie with the pastry and trim to fit, putting aside any unused pastry. Press all around the rim with a fork to seal. Make shapes or letters with the extra pastry and use them to decorate the top of the pie. Cut a small hole in the top to let the steam escape and brush the top all over with the beaten egg. Place in the oven for 30 minutes or until the pastry is golden brown. Check after 20 minutes and if it looks like it might burn cover with foil.

I like to serve this pie with herby couscous and baked tomatoes.

Tip: If you can't find cumin puff pastry, roll 2 teaspoons of cumin seeds into regular puff pastry.

Charlie is my kids' fantastic stepmum and has known them almost all of their lives. I know they are always happy and well looked after when they are with her. Thank you Charlie.

LAMB, CARROT & FRUIT JUICE PIE
by Charlie Willcock

SERVES 4

You will need 4 individual pie dishes

2 tbsp olive oil

2 lamb neck fillets, about 500g (1lb), cut into chunks

salt and freshly ground black pepper

1 large onion, chopped

300ml (10fl oz) fresh chicken stock

a splash of red wine

300ml (10fl oz) fresh apple and cranberry juice

400g (14oz) tin organic chopped tomatoes

1 tbsp organic tomato purée

a couple of splashes of Worcestershire sauce

½ tsp Tabasco sauce

500g (1lb) Chanteney carrots, trimmed and halved

300g (10oz) good-quality butter puff pastry

Heat the olive oil in a pan. Add the lamb chunks to the pan and fry them, seasoning with salt, until browned all over. Add the onion to the pan and fry until soft. Add the stock, wine and fruit juice. Cover the pan with a lid, turn up the heat and bring the mixture to the boil. Once boiling, remove the lid and allow it to simmer over a gentle heat for 2 hours.

After the 2 hours has passed, pour in the tinned tomatoes, tomato purée, Worcestershire sauce and the Tabasco. Then add the carrots and continue to simmer for 1 hour, allowing the liquid to reduce by about half.

Preheat the oven to 220°C (425°F/Gas 7). Remove the pan from the heat and season the mixture to taste with salt and pepper. Allow it to cool before pouring it into four individual pie dishes.

Divide the pastry into four, then roll out each piece on a floured board until large enough to cover the pie. Wet the edge of the pie dishes with a little water, lay the pastry on top and press around the edges with your thumb to seal. Trim off any excess pastry with a sharp knife. Cut a small hole in the tops to let the steam escape. Place in the oven and bake for 25 minutes.

My daughter Coco refused to eat shepherd's pie until she helped me make one; now she loves it. Kids are strange.

SHEPHERD'S PIE

SERVES 6

FOR THE FILLING:

2 tbsp olive oil

a knob of butter

1 red onion, chopped

2 carrots, peeled and chopped

1 large stick celery, chopped

150g (5oz) chestnut mushrooms, chopped

½ tsp dried thyme

salt and freshly ground black pepper

400g (14oz) lamb mince

2 cloves garlic, chopped

1 handful fresh flat leaf parsley, chopped

Place the oil and butter in a large pan with a lid over a medium heat. Add the onion and gently fry for 5 minutes. Add the carrots, celery, mushrooms and thyme, and season. Stir through and continue frying gently for another 15 minutes, stirring from time to time.

Add the lamb mince to the pan, breaking it up into large chunks with a wooden spoon. Then add the garlic and parsley and stir them through. Fry the mixture until all the meat has browned and any liquid has evaporated.

Stir in the wine, tinned tomatoes, Worcestershire sauce and tomato purée and stir. Cover the pan and allow it to simmer for 1 hour. Check that the mixture is not burning, sticking or drying out and stir it occasionally, adding a little water if the mixture becomes too dry. Once it is done, taste and season again if necessary.

Preheat the oven to 220°C (425°F/Gas 7). Meanwhile, prepare the mash by boiling the potatoes in plenty of salted water until they are very soft when poked with a sharp knife. Drain the spuds and mash them. I use a mouli (pictured on page 105), which makes a lovely lump-free mash. Stir through the milk and butter. You may need a bit more or less milk but you want to end up with a fairly soft mash. Season with salt (you may need more than you think).

1 small glass red wine
(about 150ml / 5fl oz)

400g (14oz) tin plum
tomatoes

½ tbsp Worcestershire sauce

1 tbsp tomato purée

FOR THE MASH:

6 medium-sized Maris Piper
potatoes, peeled and cubed

75ml (2½fl oz) milk

50g (2oz) butter, plus extra
for dotting onto the mash

When your mixture has simmered for an hour, pour it into your pie dish. Cover the mixture with the mash, then use a fork to rough the surface of the mash into small peaks, which will become lovely and crispy. Dot the mash with butter all over. Place the pie dish in the oven and bake for 35 minutes or until the top is golden.

Serve with buttered peas.

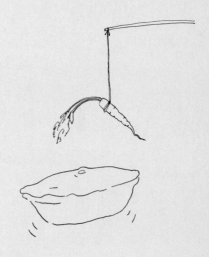

With its deliciously rich gravy and meltingly tender meat, this is a truly comforting pie that will fill your belly and put a smile on your face.

SPICED LAMB WITH BEANS

SERVES 6

FOR THE FILLING:

1 kg (2lb 4oz) lamb, either leg or shoulder, cut into 4cm (1½in) chunks

salt and freshly ground black pepper

2 tbsp olive oil

a knob of butter

2 red onions, chopped

3 cloves garlic, chopped

1 tsp paprika

1 tsp ground cumin

1 tsp crushed dried chillies

1 small glass white wine (about 150ml / 5fl oz)

400g (14oz) tin plum tomatoes

400g (14oz) tin borlotti beans, drained

1 tbsp golden caster sugar

FOR THE MASH:

5 large Desirée potatoes, peeled and cubed

125g (4oz) butter

75ml (2½fl oz) milk

Season the lamb with salt and pepper. Heat the oil in a large pan over a high heat and fry the lamb in batches until browned, then set aside.

Reduce the heat, melt the butter in the pan and throw in the onions. Give them a stir and let them gently fry for about 15 minutes. Stir in the garlic. After a couple of minutes, stir in the spices, then pour in the wine. Scrape the bottom of the pan with a wooden spoon to blend the spices with the wine. Let the mixture simmer for 5 minutes and then return the meat and its juices to the pan. Add the tomatoes and give it all a good stir. Leave it to gently bubble away for 1½ hours. Check it occasionally to make sure it is not burning or sticking and give it a stir. If it looks too dry, add a little water. Add the beans and sugar to the pot. Taste and season accordingly with salt and pepper. Remove from the heat. Spoon the mixture into a pie dish and set aside.

Preheat the oven to 220°C (425°F/Gas 7). Meanwhile, boil the potatoes in plenty of salted water for about 15 minutes or until they are very tender when poked with a sharp knife. Drain well and mash with the butter, milk and plenty of salt. I use a mouli (pictured on page 105), which makes a wonderful lump-free mash.

Spoon the mash all over the top of the pie, smooth with the back of your spoon, leaving no holes, then use a fork or the back of the spoon to rough the surface of the mash into small peaks, which will become lovely and brown with crispy bits. Place it in the oven and bake for 20 minutes or until crisp and golden.

I like to serve this pie with braised fennel.

This is one of my stepmum's pies from her book, "Classic Conran". It is eaten cold in slices and is made in the same way as a pork pie with a sturdy crust. She is a sensational cook (and a wonderful person), and her lunches are legendary.

HAM & CHICKEN PIE *by Vicki Conran*

SERVES 6

You will need either a 2-litre (3½-pint) pie mould (looks like a loaf tin with sides that flip down) or a 2-litre (3½-pint) springform cake tin

FOR THE FILLING:

250g (9oz) pork belly fat, chopped

200g (7oz) chicken thigh meat, chopped

1 handful each fresh parsley, tarragon and chervil, finely chopped

salt and freshly ground black pepper

50ml (1¾fl oz) cold strong chicken stock

250g (9oz) gammon, cut into strips

250g (9oz) chicken breast, cut into strips

ingredients continued

In a large bowl, mix the pork fat, chicken thigh meat, herbs, salt, pepper and cold chicken stock. Set it aside and make the pastry.

To make the hot water crust, place the lard and the water into a saucepan and heat gently. When the lard has melted, bring to the boil and immediately tip in the flour and salt. Mix it well with a wooden spoon to bring the pastry together. Remove from the heat and cover the pan with a tea towel until the pastry dough is cool enough to handle.

Preheat the oven to 200°C (400°F/Gas 6). Leaving one-quarter of the pastry covered and warm, roll out the larger piece. Place it into a hinged pie mould or springform cake tin. Line the tin with the pastry, which will be malleable enough to press up the sides with your fingers. The thicker you make the pastry, the stronger the pie shell will be.

Put alternate layers of the chopped meat, gammon and chicken breast strips into the pie, pressing down as you go. Roll out the remaining quarter of the pastry to make a lid.

Moisten the edges of the pie with a little water and cover it with the lid, pressing the edges together to seal. Cut a hole in the centre of the lid to let the steam escape and trim the edges of the pie; flute them if you like with your fingers or the tines of a fork.

recipe continued

Ham & Chicken Pie (continued)

FOR THE HOT WATER CRUST:

160g (5½oz) lard

250ml (9fl oz) water

450g (1lb) plain flour

½ tsp salt

1 egg yolk, beaten with 1 tbsp milk

JELLIED STOCK:

300ml (10fl oz) chicken stock (home-made or the best you can lay your mitts on)

½ sachet of gelatine

Brush the pie with some of the beaten egg yolk and milk. Place the pie in the oven and bake for 30 minutes. Reduce the heat to 170°C (325°F/Gas 3), and cook the pie for a further 1½ hours. If the top begins to look too brown, cover with some foil.

Take the pie out of the oven and very carefully remove the tin. Brush the sides of the pie with the egg wash and put it back in the oven on a baking sheet for 10 to 15 minutes to brown the sides. Remove it from the oven and allow to cool.

To make the jellied stock, warm up the stock in a small pan and sprinkle in the gelatine, stirring until the gelatine has dissolved. Allow to cool slightly. Then, using a small funnel, carefully pour it into the pie through the hole in the lid. This fills the gaps between the filling and the pastry that occur due to the shrinkage of the meat during cooking. Refrigerate the pie for 24 hours before eating.

Serve with pickled walnuts, pickled onions and Little Gem lettuce with a good dressing. Ideal as a starter, a picnic or lunch alfresco.

This makes a nice firm pie, perfect for carting about, and is delicious warm or cold. It is based on a flan made by the lovely Anna, my friend Nick Lee's mum, in the Swiss Alps. We ate it on New Year's Day.

HAM & CHEESE PICNIC PIE

SERVES 8

You will need a 27cm (11in) round flan tin

2 tbsp olive oil

a knob of butter

1 onion, chopped

2 leeks, chopped

400g (14oz) shortcrust pastry, made with 180g (6½oz) plain flour and 100g (3½oz) butter (see page 14–15)

250g (9oz) piece of cooked ham in a thick slice

3 eggs and 1 extra egg yolk

50ml (1¾fl oz) double cream

300g (10oz) Emmental cheese, grated

salt and freshly ground black pepper

Preheat the oven to 220°C (425°F/Gas 7). In a large pan, heat the oil and butter. Add the onion and gently fry it for 5 minutes. Add the leeks and fry them for 10 minutes or until they are soft.

Roll out two-thirds of the pastry on a floured board, to a thickness of about 3mm/⅛in. Grease the flan tin and line it with the pastry. Prick the base with a fork about 15 times, and then cover it with foil. Place it in the oven and bake for 15 minutes. Remove the foil and then bake for a further 5 minutes until golden. Remove the pie case from the oven and allow to cool.

Chop the ham into 1cm (½in) cubes and set aside. Beat the eggs and cream together, and mix in the cheese, leeks and onion, and ham. Season the mixture with salt and plenty of pepper. Pour it into the baked pastry case.

Roll out the rest of the pastry into a disc big enough to cover the pie. Lay the disc over the pie dish and trim to fit, decorating the top with any excess pastry. Cut a small hole in the top to let the steam escape. Place the pie in the oven and bake for 15 minutes, then remove from the oven and cover with foil. Bake for a further 10 minutes. Allow the pie to cool slightly before turning it onto a plate. To do this, cover the top of the pie with a plate, flip it over, lift off the flan tin and then flip it carefully back onto another plate.

I like to serve this pie with a tomato salad.

Pork has a wonderful affinity with both apples and prunes. If you like tender pork with a little sweetness, you'll love this pie.

PORK & PRUNE WITH APPLE MASH

SERVES 6

FOR THE FILLING:

4 tbsp olive oil

500g (1lb) pork leg meat, cut into 3cm (1in) cubes

a knob of butter

1 large onion, sliced

3 cloves garlic, chopped

1 tsp each salt and freshly ground black pepper

75g (2¾oz) demerara sugar

2 tsp dried oregano

1 tsp dried thyme

500ml (18fl oz) dry cider

200g (7oz) prunes, stoned and ready to eat

1 small handful fresh sage leaves, chopped

Heat the oil in a large pan with a lid over a high heat and quickly fry the pork until browned. You may need to do this in batches. When all the meat has been browned, set aside.

Turn down the heat, add the butter, onion and garlic and season with the salt and pepper. Slowly cook for 10 minutes, stirring occasionally, until softened. Be careful not to let the onion and garlic brown.

Return the pork to the pan and stir in the sugar, oregano and thyme. Allow the sugar to melt, then add the cider, prunes and sage. Put on the lid and allow to simmer for 1 hour. Check occasionally to ensure it is not sticking to the pan and stir it through from time to time. After an hour, remove the lid and simmer for a further 20 minutes to allow the sauce to thicken.

Preheat the oven to 180°C (350°F/Gas 4). Meanwhile, prepare the mash. Put the apples in a small pan with the water, cover and cook over a low heat for 5 minutes. Remove the lid and cook for a further 5 minutes. Remove from the heat and mash the apples lightly with a fork. Set them aside.

Boil the potatoes in a large pan of salted water until they are tender when poked with a sharp knife. I use a mouli (pictured on page 105), which makes a lovely lump-free mash. Drain and mash until very smooth. Then stir in the butter, milk and apples, and season the mash.

FOR THE MASH:

500g (1lb) Granny Smith
 apples, peeled, cored
 and cut into 8 slices

2 tbsp water

900g (2lb) Maris Piper
 potatoes, peeled and
 cubed

salt and freshly ground
 black pepper

100g (3½oz) butter

75ml (2½fl oz) milk

Pour the pork mixture into a pie dish and spoon the apple mash evenly over the top, making sure there are no holes but leaving rough small peaks that will crisp and brown nicely. Place the pie in the oven and bake it for 25 minutes until golden on top.

I like to serve this pie with purple sprouting broccoli.

This is another excellent recipe from my development chef, Robert. The polenta gives the pastry a fantastic grainy texture. Any harshness in the Stilton softens to make a rich and creamy sauce.

PORK & STILTON WITH POLENTA PASTRY

by Robert Barker

SERVES 4

FOR THE PASTRY:

110g (4oz) butter, chilled

140g (5oz) plain flour

55g (2oz) polenta

a pinch of salt

2 egg yolks

2 tbsp chopped fresh herbs (parsley, chives and tarragon)

2 tbsp cold water

1 egg, beaten

To make the pastry, cut the butter into cubes and put it into a food processor with the flour, polenta and salt. Using the cutting blade, blitz until it resembles fine breadcrumbs. Add the egg yolks and herbs, then add the water a little at a time. Pulse the mixture until it binds together into a ball. Scoop it out of the food processor and dust with flour. Form the dough into a thick disc. Cover with cling film and chill for a minimum of 1 hour in the fridge. Allow the pastry to come back to room temperature before using.

To make the filling, heat the oil in a large frying pan over a high heat and fry the pork until browned all over, then reduce the heat, stir through the flour and cook for 3 minutes. In a separate large pan, gently melt the butter, then lightly fry the onion for 5 minutes. Add the garlic and continue frying for a further 3 minutes or until soft. Pour in the wine and simmer until reduced by half. Add the stock, mushrooms and pork, and bring to the boil, then reduce the heat and simmer for 1 hour. After this time, stir in the cream, mustard and cheese and cook for a further 30 minutes. Finally, season with salt and pepper and stir through the parsley.

FOR THE FILLING:

2 tbsp olive oil

600g (1lb 5oz) shoulder
of pork, diced

20g (¾oz) plain flour

20g (¾oz) butter

1 small onion, diced
(about 80g / 3oz)

1 clove garlic, diced

300ml (10fl oz) white wine

150ml (5fl oz) chicken stock

80g (3oz) flat mushrooms,
sliced

60ml (2fl oz) double cream

½ tbsp Dijon mustard

70g (2½oz) Stilton cheese,
crumbled

salt and freshly ground
black pepper

1 handful fresh flat leaf
parsley, chopped

Preheat the oven to 180°C (350°F/Gas 4). Spoon the pork mixture into a pie dish. Brush the rim of the pie dish with a little of the beaten egg. Roll out the pastry and cover the pie with it, then cut the pastry to size and press with a fork to seal around the rim. Cut the unused pastry into shapes or letters and decorate the top. Brush the top with beaten egg and cut a small hole in the top to let the steam escape. Place in the oven and bake for 30 minutes.

Serve with root vegetable mash.

I remember my mum making these when I was a kid. I have no idea if mine are anything like the ones I loved all those years ago, but they have gone down very well with everyone who has tried them.

Sausage & Apricot Parcels

MAKES 9 PARCELS

salt and freshly ground black pepper

1 large Savoy cabbage

a knob of butter

350g (12oz) calves' liver, cut into slices

2 tbsp brandy

½ medium white loaf of bread, crusts removed (about 200g/7oz)

rind of 1 unwaxed lemon, grated

50g (2oz) dried apricots, chopped

1½ tsp dried sage, crumbled

1½ tsp dried thyme, crumbled

3 excellent sausages, skin removed

Fill a big lidded pot with water. Add a large pinch of salt and bring to the boil. Meanwhile, carefully strip nine of the largest leaves from the cabbage, keeping them whole. Cut out the thickest part of the midrib. Plunge the leaves into the boiling water, cover the pot and boil for 3 to 4 minutes. Meanwhile, fill the sink with cold water, then plunge the boiled leaves into the cold water once cooked. Dry them thoroughly with kitchen paper and set aside.

Preheat the oven to 220°C (425°F/Gas 7). Place the butter in a frying pan over a medium heat. Fry the liver on both sides until it just changes colour. Pour in the brandy and turn up the heat. Shake the pan over the heat until the brandy has evaporated, then take the pan off the heat and set it aside.

Whiz the bread in a food processor until you have soft breadcrumbs. Pour into a large bowl and set them aside.

Chop the liver into little cubes, and throw them into the bowl of breadcrumbs along with any juice from the frying pan. Then add the lemon rind, apricots, herbs and sausagemeat and mix them through. Season the mixture with salt and pepper. Now spread out a cabbage leaf. Place a handful of sausage and apricot mixture onto the leaf. Wrap it up like a little present and place it on a baking tray with the smooth side up. Repeat the same process for the other eight leaves. Place them in the oven and bake them for 20 minutes.

Serve the parcels with fried potatoes and mustard.

This heartening pie features one of the great combos of the world – sausage, onion and mash. I like to use fantastic Italian sausages that only contain pork and spices, with a meat content of 97%, so they are more dense than normal sausages.

Sausage & Caramelised Onion with Mash

SERVES 2

FOR THE FILLING:

4 tbsp olive oil

a knob of butter

4 large red onions, finely sliced

4 tbsp golden caster sugar

3 tbsp sherry vinegar

250ml (9fl oz) beef stock

300g (10oz) sausages, cooked and then sliced into 2cm (¾in) pieces

salt and freshly ground black pepper

FOR THE MASH:

2 large potatoes, either Maris Piper or King Edward, peeled and cubed

75ml (2½fl oz) milk

50g (2oz) butter, plus a little extra to dot onto the top of the pie

Place the oil and butter in a large casserole over a low heat. Add the onions and fry gently for 40 minutes. Stir occasionally to make sure they don't burn; they should become a soft mass.

Add the sugar and vinegar and simmer for 5 more minutes. Add the stock and simmer for a further 10 minutes until the mixture becomes thick and caramelised. Season to taste, take it off the heat and set aside.

Preheat the oven to 220°C (425°F/Gas 7). Meanwhile, boil the potatoes in plenty of salted water until they are very soft when poked with a sharp knife. Drain the potatoes and mash. I use a mouli (pictured on page 105) for a lovely lump-free mash. Stir through the milk and butter. You may need a bit more or less milk but you want to end up with a fairly soft mash. Add salt; you may find that you need more than you think.

Mix the sausage slices with the onions, then pour into a pie dish. Spoon the mash on the top in dollops to cover completely, smoothing the mash over with the back of a spoon to fill any holes. Dot the mash with butter. Place the pie in the oven and bake for 20 minutes.

I like to serve this pie with buttered cabbage.

I pinched this recipe from my mum and adapted it in trials for my pie range. It is the largest and most magnificent sausage roll you will ever taste.

SAUSAGE & MUSHROOM PIE

SERVES 4–5

450g (1lb) sausagemeat

2 cloves garlic, crushed

salt and freshly ground black pepper

¼ tsp ground nutmeg

1 handful fresh flat leaf parsley leaves, chopped

2 fresh sage leaves, finely chopped

a generous pinch of dried thyme

rind of 1 unwaxed lemon, grated

45g (1¾oz) butter

½ onion, finely chopped

340g (12oz) mushrooms, finely sliced

300g (10oz) good-quality butter puff pastry

1 egg, beaten

Preheat the oven to 220°C (425°F/Gas 7). In a bowl, mix the sausagemeat with the garlic, a little salt, pepper, nutmeg, herbs and lemon rind. Set aside.

Heat the butter in a large frying pan on a medium heat. Add the chopped onion and fry gently for 10 minutes until it becomes translucent. Add the mushrooms, season and cook gently until they are soft. Remove the pan from the heat and set aside to cool.

Roll out about two-thirds of the pastry into a rectangle measuring 30 x 20cm (12 x 8in), and lay it on a greased baking sheet. Take one-third of the sausagemeat and pat it out in the middle of the pastry, leaving a margin of about 6cm (2½in) all around. Place a layer of the mushroom mixture on top of this and press them on lightly. Keep alternating layers of sausage and mushrooms, finishing with a layer of sausage mixture. Pat it into a nicely even rectangular shape. Bring up the sides of the pastry and fold it over the filling. Cut off any excess at the corners. There should still be a rectangle of the sausage mixture visible at the top.

Roll out the remaining pastry into a rectangular lid for the pie. Cut even parallel slashes in it at 1cm (½in) intervals, leaving a margin of 1cm (½in) uncut all the way around. Brush the top lightly with a little of the beaten egg and place it, moist-side down, on top of the pie. The filling should be just visible through the slashes. To help stop the pastry breaking up while the pie is in the oven, brush all over the top of the pie with a little more beaten egg and leave to dry for 10 minutes, then brush it with egg a second time. Leave to dry for a further 5 to 10 minutes.

Place the roll in the oven. Bake it for 15 minutes, then turn down the oven temperature to 180°C (350°F/Gas 4). Bake it for a further 30 minutes and then remove it from the oven. The pie will be golden, and the top will have opened out and risen to show the filling. Leave to cool (if possible overnight) before eating.

This pie is great for a picnic. I like to serve it in thickish slices with a herby green salad, potato salad, chunks of bread, cheeses and chutney.

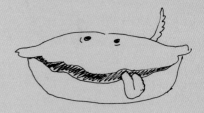

A firm and tasty pie with lovely smoked bacon bits.
This is best eaten warm, but it is pretty good cold too.

POTATO & BACON PIE

SERVES 4

You will need a 23cm (9in)
round tart tin

a splash of olive oil

6 rashers smoked back
bacon

300g (10oz) shortcrust
pastry, made with 200g
(7oz) plain flour and
100g (3½oz) butter
(see pages 14–15)

2 medium baking potatoes,
peeled and thinly sliced

2 cloves garlic, finely
chopped

150ml (5fl oz) double cream

1 handful fresh flat leaf
parsley, chopped

1 tsp mixed dried rosemary
and thyme, crushed

salt and freshly ground
black pepper

Parmesan cheese the size
of a walnut, grated

Preheat the oven to 220°C (425°F/Gas 7). Pour the olive oil in a
frying pan over a medium-high heat. Add the bacon and fry until it
has browned and is beginning to become crisp on both sides. Take
the pan off the heat, remove the bacon and set aside. Once cool
enough to handle, slice the bacon roughly into 1cm (½in) strips.

Grease the tart tin well with butter. Roll out the pastry on a floured
board so it is large enough to line the tin. Lay it in the tart tin and
prick the base with a fork all over about 15 times. Trim the excess
pastry, cover the tin with foil and place it in the oven. After 15
minutes, remove the pastry from the oven and take off the foil. Press
the base of the pastry down if it has risen and pop it back into the
oven for a further 5 minutes.

While the pastry is baking, rinse the potato slices in a colander until
the water runs clear. Drain the potatoes, dry them well with a tea
towel and put them in a large bowl. Mix them well with the garlic,
cream, herbs and bacon. Season with plenty of freshly ground black
pepper and salt.

Pack the potato mixture into the pastry case so it is nice and
compact, and pour in any sauce remaining in the bowl. Sprinkle the
grated Parmesan over the top, cover the pie with foil and put it in
the oven. After 45 minutes, remove the foil, put the pie back into the
oven and bake for a further 15 minutes.

I like to serve this with a tomato and basil salad and chilled white
wine.

I spent hours as a child pretending to be the unfortunate sister of a desperate pioneer in a disintegrating wagon, travelling west across America to a distant promised land. This is the pie I would have cooked if we had ever made it there. Like my childhood games, it is a delicious fiction.

BACON & SOUTHERN SPOONBREAD PIE

SERVES 4

FOR THE FILLING:

550g (1lb 4oz) cured pork loin (boiling bacon)

1 leek

2 sticks celery

1 small onion, peeled and halved

1 carrot, peeled

2 bay leaves

15g (½oz) butter

1 tbsp plain flour

150ml (5fl oz) milk

150ml (5fl oz) double cream

a pinch of ground nutmeg

1 large handful fresh parsley leaves, chopped

2 sprigs each fresh tarragon, parsley, rosemary and thyme

14 pearl (or 'button') onions, peeled

Put the cured pork loin (boiling bacon) in a pan over a medium heat. Add the leek, celery, halved onion, carrot and one bay leaf. Cover with water and allow to simmer gently for 45 minutes.

Meanwhile, heat the butter in a medium-sized pan. Add the flour and let it gently bubble for a couple of minutes. Pour in the milk and cream and whisk vigorously until you have a smooth sauce. Add the nutmeg, herbs, pearl onions and the remaining bay leaf. Cook gently for 10 minutes, stirring now and again. Ladle in some of the stock from the pork if it is a bit too thick at this point. Continue cooking the sauce for a further 20 minutes.

Take the pork out of the stock and leave to cool for at least 10 minutes. Then trim off the outside, cut the pork into largish chunks and stir into the sauce. Keep aside till needed. Chuck out the vegetables and bay leaf from the stock and carry on boiling for 30 minutes; you end up with a fantastic golden broth. Any leftover broth can be kept in the fridge or freezer in an airtight container and used in place of stock in soups, gravy, risotto, sauces, stews or even pies.

FOR THE SPOONBREAD:

150g (5oz) instant polenta

1 tsp salt

½ tbsp demerera sugar

1 tsp bicarbonate of soda

1 tsp baking powder

30g (14oz) butter

1 mild dried red chilli, crushed

2 eggs, beaten

Preheat the oven to 220°C (425°F/Gas 7). Then make the spoonbread topping by first mixing together the polenta, salt, sugar, bicarbonate of soda and baking powder in a largish bowl. In a small pan, heat the butter and 400ml (14fl oz) of the broth over a medium heat until the butter melts. Add the chilli and remove the pan from the heat to allow it to cool slightly. Mix the eggs into the polenta mixture, followed by the warm broth. It should now be the consistency of very thick custard. Pour the ham and sauce into the pie dish, then top with the spoonbread. Bake for 20 minutes. Try serving with buttery corn-on-the-cob.

Tweety Pies

Packed with magnificent flavours and juicy textures, this is a fine pie to eat at a table or under a tree. I like to serve this pie with rice and buttered spinach

SPANISH CHICKEN PIE

SERVES 6

8 chicken thighs

salt and freshly ground black pepper

2 tbsp olive oil

a knob of butter

2 small red onions, chopped

2 sticks celery, chopped

2 red peppers, cored, deseeded and sliced

1 fennel bulb, trimmed and sliced

8 cloves garlic, chopped

½ tsp saffron threads

2 tsp paprika

1 large glass red wine (about 300ml/10fl oz)

400g (14oz) tin plum tomatoes

FOR THE PASTRY:

100g (3½oz) prepared suet, such as Atora

200g (7oz) self-raising flour

4 tbsp white wine

a large pinch of salt

1 egg, beaten

Season the chicken with salt and pepper. Heat the oil in a large pot and fry the chicken pieces until they are slightly brown. Remove from the pot and set aside for the moment. Add the butter to the pot and stir in the onions, celery, peppers and fennel. Leave them to stew gently for 15 minutes, stirring occasionally. Mix in the garlic, saffron and paprika. After 2 minutes, pour in the wine and tomatoes. Season with a pinch of salt and a few grinds of black pepper.

Return the chicken to the pot and simmer for 30 minutes, stirring from time to time to make sure it does not stick. Allow the mixture to cool and then take the chicken pieces out of the sauce.

Preheat the oven to 220°C (425°F/Gas 7). Pull the chicken meat from the bones with your fingers, discarding the skin and bones. Cut the meat into bite-sized pieces and stir it back into the sauce. Season the mixture to taste and then pour it into a pie dish. Set the dish aside.

Make the pastry by mixing the suet, flour, white wine and salt together in a large bowl until you have a soft dough. Add a little more flour if the dough is sticky, or wine if it is too dry. Knead the dough for a couple of minutes until it becomes smooth and a little elastic.

Roll out the pastry so it will be big enough to cover the pie dish. Brush the rim of the dish with a little of the beaten egg and place the pastry over the pie. Trim the edges and brush the top of the pastry with more egg. Press the edges down using the tines of a fork. Cut pastry shapes from the extra pastry and decorate the top of the pie. Cut a hole in the top to let the steam escape and brush all over with more of the egg. Bake for 30 minutes. Check after 15 minutes. If the pastry is turning golden, cover with foil.

I love boiled eggs in pies; they add a great texture and flavour. You can substitute the boiled chicken for leftover roast chicken, using a good-quality chicken stock for the sauce.

CHICKEN & EGG PIE

SERVES 4

1 small chicken, about 1kg (2lb 4oz)

1 onion, peeled and halved

1 large carrot, peeled

1 leek, chopped into large chunks

1 stick celery, halved

1 bunch fresh parsley stalks, either flat leaf or curly

25g (1oz) butter

1 tbsp plain flour

150ml (5fl oz) double cream

salt and freshly ground black pepper

4 boiled eggs, peeled and cut into quarters

150g (5oz) ham, cut into 1cm (½in) cubes

300g (10oz) good-quality butter puff pastry, at room temperature

1 egg, beaten

Put the chicken in a large pot with the onion, carrot, leek, celery and parsley stalks. Cover with water and gently simmer for an hour. Don't let it boil; the liquid should just quiver. After an hour, remove the chicken to cool. Chuck out the vegetables and parsley stalks, but leave the stock in the pan.

Turn up the heat under the stock and boil rapidly for 1 hour or until it is about one-third of its original volume. In another large pan, gently melt the butter, stir in the flour and let it sizzle for a couple of minutes. Strain the stock into the butter and flour and give it a good whisk. Let it simmer for 20 minutes or until you have a thickish sauce, whisking it from time to time. Once you have a lovely velvety sauce, whisk in the cream. Remove from the heat and season to taste.

Preheat the oven to 220°C (425°F/Gas 7). Separate the chicken meat from the bones and skin. Cut the meat into bite-sized chunks and bin the bones and skin. Stir the eggs, chicken chunks and ham cubes through the sauce, then fill a pie dish with the mixture and set aside.

Roll out the pastry into a piece large enough to cover the pie dish. Brush the rim of the pie dish with a little of the beaten egg and cover the pie with the pastry. Cut the pastry to size and press down on the rim with a fork to seal. Brush the top with a little more beaten egg and decorate with the unused pastry, rolled out and cut into shapes. Cut a small hole in the top to let the steam escape and brush over once more with the egg. Bake the pie in the oven for 20 minutes.

I like to serve this with mashed potatoes and buttered carrots tossed with a little chopped fresh tarragon.

This is also a great pie to make with leftover chicken or turkey. My mum would make it at Christmas and it was always one of my favourite dishes.

DEVILLED CHICKEN PIE

SERVES 6

FOR THE FILLING:

1 kg (2lb 4oz) skinless, boneless chicken breasts, cut into 4cm (1½in) cubes

1 tsp dried rosemary and thyme, crushed

salt and freshly ground black pepper

2 tbsp olive oil

2 tbsp Worcestershire sauce

6 anchovy fillets, pounded to a paste

300ml (10fl oz) double cream (medium pot)

1 tsp anchovy sauce

1 tsp paprika

FOR THE MASH:

4 largish Desirée potatoes, peeled and cubed

1 small wine glass milk (about 150ml/5fl oz)

100g (3½oz) butter

Preheat the oven to 220°C (425°F/Gas 7). Coat the chicken cubes in the herbs and season with salt and pepper. Heat the oil in a large frying pan. Lay the chicken in the pan in one layer and fry briskly, turning until it changes from pink to white; you may need to do this in batches. The chicken does not need to be cooked through, just sealed on the outside. Put the chicken to one side on a plate until needed.

Mix the Worcestershire sauce and anchovies together in a bowl until blended. Pour in the cream and anchovy sauce and sprinkle in the paprika. Mix it well and set it aside.

Now make the mash by boiling the potatoes in plenty of salted water until they are very soft when poked with a sharp knife. Drain the spuds and mash. I use a mouli (pictured on page 105) to make a lovely lump-free mash. Stir through the milk and butter; you may need a bit more or less milk to end up with a fairly soft mash. Add some salt; you'll probably need quite a bit.

Fill a pie dish with the chicken and creamy anchovy sauce, and mix through. Top the pie dish with the mash, spooning the mash all over the top. Smooth over any holes with the back of your spoon then, take a fork and rough the surface of the mash into peaks, which will become brown and crispy. Pop it in the oven and bake for 30 minutes or until golden.

I like to serve this pie with roast vegetables such as parsnips, sweet potatoes, carrots and butternut squash.

Another recipe from Charlie, my kids' stepmum. Their dad, Alex, has an allergy to cows' milk, so she invented this pie for him. The coconut milk also adds a wonderful creamy texture and an exotic flavour.

CHICKEN & ASPARAGUS WITH COCONUT MILK *by Charlie Willcock*

SERVES 4

You will need 4 individual pie dishes

2 tbsp olive oil

4 skinless, boneless organic chicken breasts, cubed

salt and freshly ground black pepper

1 onion, chopped

2 bunches of organic asparagus (about 400g / 14oz in total) or you could use baby leeks and/or broccoli

300g (10oz) good-quality butter puff pastry

FOR THE BÉCHAMEL SAUCE:

50g (2oz) butter

2 tbsp plain flour

1½ x 400ml (14fl oz) tins organic coconut milk (600ml or just over 1 pint)

Preheat the oven to 220°C (425°F/Gas 7). Heat the oil in a pan. Place the chicken cubes in the oil and brown, stirring occasionally. Season with salt and then add the onion to the pan. Fry the onion until soft.

Meanwhile, cut the woody ends off the asparagus and throw them away. Slice the remaining stems diagonally into thirds. Add these to the pan and remove from the heat.

Now make the béchamel sauce, substituting coconut milk for cows' milk. Melt the butter in a pan, strin in the flour and let it bubble for a couple of minutes. Gradually add the coconut milk, stirring and cooking until it has thickened. Season the sauce with salt and pepper.

Pour the coconut sauce over the chicken and stir gently. Pour the mixture into four individual pie dishes. Roll out the puff pastry and cut it into four pieces that will fit over the pie dishes. Brush the rim of the dishes with water and lay the puff pastry over the top. Trim away any extra pastry and seal the pastry onto the rim by pressing all around with your thumbs. Cut a small hole in the tops to let the steam escape. Bake in the oven for 25 minutes.

Serve with rice.

The lovely Sunil Vijayakar helped to develop this for my pie range. It may seem like an odd combination but it is divine and won gold in The Great Taste Awards, the food equivalent of the Oscars.

CHICKEN, OLIVE & PRESERVED LEMON PIE

SERVES 4

4 tbsp olive oil

a knob of butter

4 leeks, halved lengthways, thinly sliced

1 tsp ground cumin

4 small (plum-sized) preserved lemons, rinsed and roughly chopped

1kg (2lb 4oz) chicken thighs, bones and skin removed and cut into bite-sized pieces

2 tbsp plain flour

250ml (9fl oz) good-quality fresh chicken stock

200g (7oz) green olives, pitted and roughly chopped

3 tbsp fresh flat leaf parsley, chopped

300g (10oz) good-quality butter puff pastry

1 egg, beaten

salt and freshly ground black pepper

Heat half the oil and the butter in a large casserole. Add the leeks and cook for 5 minutes until soft. Add the cumin, stir it through and then fry for another minute. Stir the lemons into the mixture and then remove the casserole from the heat and set aside.

In a frying pan, heat the remaining oil and cook the chicken in batches until it has browned. This will take about 5 minutes. Then put all the chicken and juices in the casserole with the leeks and lemons. Sprinkle the flour over everything and stir it in. Allow to cook for 3 minutes, and then gradually stir in the chicken stock.

Bring the mixture to the boil, reduce the heat and allow to simmer gently for approximately 7 minutes or until it has thickened slightly. Stir in the chopped olives and parsley. Remove the casserole from the heat and allow it to cool completely.

Once cooled, spoon the chicken mixture into a pie dish and preheat the oven to 220°C (425°F/Gas 7). Roll out the pastry into a piece that is large enough to cover the dish. Brush the rim of the pie dish with a little of the beaten egg. Cover the pie with the pastry and cut to size. Press around the rim with a fork or your thumb to seal, putting aside any unused pastry. Cut the unused pastry into shapes to decorate the top of the pie. Cut a hole in the top to let the steam escape, and brush the pie all over with the egg. Place it in the oven and cook it for 25 minutes until golden.

I like to serve this pie with buttered basmati rice and green beans.

Robert made this excellent pie. He is a development chef writing recipes for large-scale production. He has to be very precise in his line of work. No dollops, scoops or handfuls for him.

CHICKEN, LENTIL, SPINACH & SMOKED BACON *by Robert Barker*

SERVES 4

20ml (¾fl oz) olive oil

650g (1lb 7oz) chicken thigh meat, diced

40g (1½oz) pancetta, diced

50g (2oz) onions, diced

30g (1¼oz) carrot, diced

20g (¾oz) celery, diced

3g (⅒oz) garlic, diced (equivalent to 1 small clove)

15g (½oz) plain flour

50ml (1¾fl oz) white wine

300ml (10fl oz) chicken stock

70g (2½oz) Puy lentils, cooked

70ml (2½fl oz) double cream

75g (2¾oz) spinach

3g (⅒oz) fresh flat leaf parsley, chopped (equivalent to 1 tbsp)

salt and freshly ground black pepper

375g (13oz) good-quality butter puff pastry

1 egg, beaten

Preheat the oven to 180°C (350°F/Gas 4). Heat the oil in a large casserole over a medium heat. Place the chicken, pancetta, onions, carrot, celery and garlic in the hot oil and brown them. Add the flour, stir through and fry for a further 5 minutes.

Add the wine and allow it to reduce by half. Then add the chicken stock and allow it to simmer for 20 minutes. Now add the lentils, cream, spinach and parsley. Cook for a further 3 to 4 minutes. Season with salt and pepper, then spoon the chicken mixture into a pie dish.

Roll out the pastry into a piece that is large enough to cover the pie dish. Brush the rim of the pie dish with a little of the beaten egg. Lay the pastry over the pie and cut it to size, putting aside any unused pastry. Press down around the rim using a fork to seal. Brush the pastry with a little more of the egg. Cut the unused pastry into shapes and use to decorate the pie. Cut a small hole in the top of the pie to let the steam escape and brush with egg. Place in the oven and cook for 30 to 35 minutes.

This pie is a meal in itself but a side salad is always a good idea.

Chicken and leeks are lovely together. This is a real comfort pie, which is great for all the family. I've suggested serving it with roast potatoes, since that makes it my friend Nicki L's favourite meal. Her granny would make her chicken pie and roast potatoes as a special treat.

Chicken with Leeks & Cream

SERVES 6

8 chicken thighs

1 tbsp olive oil

½ tsp dried rosemary, crumbled

salt and freshly ground black pepper

a knob of butter

3 leeks, chopped

1 tbsp plain flour

1 small glass white wine (about 150ml / 5fl oz)

150ml (5fl oz) chicken stock

150ml (5 fl oz) double cream

1 large handful fresh tarragon leaves, chopped

375g (13oz) good-quality butter puff pastry

1 egg, beaten

Preheat the oven to 220°C (425°F/Gas 7). Put the chicken in a roasting dish, drizzle over the oil and season with the rosemary, salt and pepper. Place it in the oven and roast for 30 minutes. Remove from the oven and allow to cool.

Meanwhile, melt the butter in a large casserole. Add the leeks and fry gently for a couple of minutes. Sprinkle the flour over the leeks and stir for a minute or so. Whisk in the wine and stock, and simmer for 15 minutes. Then stir in the cream and continue simmering for a further 5 minutes.

Cut the chicken into bite-sized pieces and discard the skin and bones. Stir the chicken into the sauce, together with all the juice from the roasting dish. Add the tarragon, then taste and season accordingly. Pour the mixture into a pie dish and set aside.

Roll out the pastry to a size large enough to cover the pie. Brush the edges of the dish with a little of the beaten egg, and cover the pie dish with the pastry. Trim the edges, putting aside any unused pastry. Press down along the rim of the pie dish with the tines of a fork. Make shapes out of the leftover pastry and use them to decorate the top of the pie. Cut a small hole in the top of the pie to let the steam escape, and brush it all over with egg. Place the pie in the oven and bake for 20 minutes.

Serve with roast potatoes and runner beans.

This is a no-nonsense chicken and gravy pie, a perfect dish for fussy kids, since the flavour is not challenging in any way. The mushrooms can be replaced with cooked carrots or more chicken.

CHICKEN & MUSHROOM PIE FOR LITTLE CHICKENS

SERVES 8 LITTLE CHICKS OR 4 OLD HENS

1 small chicken, about 1kg (2lb 4oz)

1 onion, peeled and halved

1 large carrot, peeled and halved

1 leek, chopped into large chunks

1 whole stick celery

1 bunch fresh parsley, either flat leaf or curly

25g (1oz) butter

1 tbsp plain flour

150g (5oz) baby button mushrooms, halved

salt and freshly ground black pepper

300g (10oz) good-quality butter puff pastry

1 egg, beaten

Put the chicken in a large pot with the onion, carrot, leek, celery and parsley, and cover with water. Simmer gently for 1 hour. Don't let it boil; the liquid should just quiver. After an hour, remove the chicken and set it aside to cool. Chuck out the vegetables and parsley, leaving just the stock in the pan.

Increase the heat under the stock and boil rapidly for 1 hour until it is about one-third of its original volume. Meanwhile, in another large pan, gently melt the butter, stir in the flour and let it bubble for a couple of minutes. Strain the stock into the butter and flour and give it a good whisk. Throw in the mushrooms and allow the stock to simmer for about 30 minutes until you have a thickish sauce, stirring it from time to time. Season to taste.

Preheat the oven to 220°C (425°F/Gas 7). Remove the chicken from the pot and separate the chicken meat from the bones and skin. Cut the meat into bite-sized chunks and bin the bones and skin. Remove the sauce from the heat and stir in the chicken chunks. Spoon the chicken mixture into a pie dish or use four individual pie dishes and set aside.

Roll out the pastry to a piece large enough to cover the pie. Brush the rim of the pie dish with a little of the beaten egg. Place the pastry over the dish and trim it to size. Press around the rim of the dish with a fork to seal. Decorate the top with the unused pastry cut into shapes. Cut a small hole in the top to let the steam escape and brush with the beaten egg. Place the pie in the oven and bake for 20 minutes.

I like to serve this pie with fried potatoes and buttered carrots.

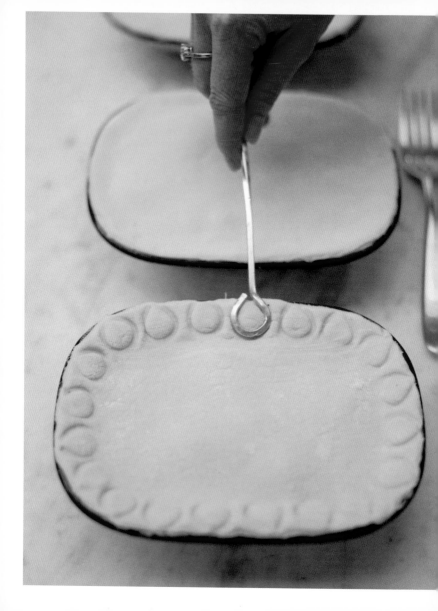

This is my idea of heaven. I had a farm in Devon a few years ago, and I discovered a secret woodland spot that in September, would be filled with chanterelles. Finding them was like discovering treasure as they glowed like gold through the moss and tasted like the food of the gods.

CREAMY CHICKEN WITH CHANTERELLE MUSHROOMS

SERVES 4

2 tbsp olive oil

500g (1lb) skinless, boneless chicken breasts, cut into 4cm (1½in) cubes

salt and freshly ground black pepper

1 tbsp fresh thyme leaves, finely chopped

25g (1oz) butter

2 leeks, white parts only, chopped

100g (3½oz) fresh chanterelles

2 cloves garlic, chopped

1 small wine glass sweet sherry (about 150ml/ 5fl oz)

284ml (10fl oz) double cream (1 medium pot)

375g (13oz) good-quality butter puff pastry

1 egg, beaten

Preheat the oven to 220°C (425°F/Gas 7). Heat the oil in a large casserole and throw in the chicken. Season and add the chopped thyme. Fry the chicken briskly on a high heat; you don't need to cook it through, just brown it all over to seal it. Remove the chicken from the pan and put to one side until needed. Turn down the heat before adding the butter and leeks to the pan. Fry them gently for 10 minutes.

Roughly chop the mushrooms and add them to the pan along with the garlic. Stir through for a couple of minutes and then turn up the heat. Pour in the sherry and boil until it evaporates.

Reduce the heat and stir in the chicken and cream. Heat through and season to taste, then pour it in a pie dish. Roll out the pastry to the thickness of about 3mm/⅛in. Brush the edges of the pie dish with a little of the beaten egg, cover the dish with the pastry and trim it to size. Press the edges down around the rim with a fork, your thumb or any ustensil that will create a decorative edge, such as the wrong end of a skewer. Decorate the pie with shapes cut from the pastry trimmings, cut a small hole in the top to let the steam escape and brush it all over with beaten egg. Place in the oven and bake for 30 minutes, checking after 15 minutes and covering with foil if it looks browned enough.

I like to serve this pie with boiled new potatoes and fine French beans.

I have used polenta to top this pie but it is also great with puff pastry, of which you would need about 300g (10oz). I usually use chicken thighs in my pies, as breast meat tends to dry out. It is not a hard and fast rule; it's just my preference.

CHICKEN WITH RED WINE & POLENTA TOP

SERVES 4

10g (¼oz) dried porcini mushrooms, soaked in a large wine glass boiling water (about 300ml/ 10fl oz)

2 tbsp olive oil

150g (5oz) bacon lardons

2 red onions, chopped

3 cloves garlic, finely chopped

1 tsp dried thyme, crumbled

6 chicken thighs

1 tbsp plain flour, seasoned with salt and pepper

1 large glass red wine (about 300ml/10fl oz), something full-bodied like a Shiraz or Merlot

1 tbsp sherry vinegar

1 tbsp soft dark brown sugar

salt and freshly ground black pepper

Put the dried porcini in a bowl and cover with the boiling water. Set aside. Pour the oil into a large casserole. Fry the bacon until starting to crisp and brown. Dump in the onions and stir through. Fry gently for 10 minutes or until the onions are soft. Add the garlic and stir it in.

Take the porcini out of the water and roughly chop them; hang onto the liquid. Add the porcini to the casserole, along with the thyme.

Coat the chicken pieces in the seasoned flour and fry with the onion, bacon and mushrooms until they start to change colour. Be sure to keep everything moving so it doesn't stick. Add the wine, mushroom liquid, the vinegar and sugar. Scrape the bottom of the pan and simmer everything gently for 30 minutes, turning the pieces of chicken over occasionally and adding a little water if it becomes too dry. After 30 minutes, allow it to cool.

Meanwhile, preheat the oven to 220°C (425°F/Gas 7) and make the polenta. Warm the milk, butter, nutmeg and salt in a pan. When the butter begins to melt, stir in the polenta. Heat until it is almost boiling, stirring continuously for 5 minutes. Remove from the heat. Stir in the rosemary and then the egg. The polenta should be the consistency of porridge, so add more milk if it is not soft enough and set aside.

FOR THE TOPPING:

600ml (1 pint) milk

100g (3½oz) butter

a pinch of ground nutmeg

a pinch of salt

100g (3½oz) instant polenta

1 tsp fresh rosemary leaves,
   finely chopped

1 egg, beaten

Then, working quickly so the polenta does not set, remove the chicken from the pot and cut the meat into bite-sized chunks, discarding the skin and bones. Put the chicken in a pie dish, and stir through the bacon and wine mixture. Pour the polenta over to cover. Place the pie in the oven and cook for 25 minutes or until golden brown.

I like to serve this pie with a big crispy, herby salad dressed with a garlic vinaigrette.

Sage is my gorgeous sister-in-law, who has been helping my brother Tom set up his Mexican restaurant. She writes the recipes and sources the strange and tasty ingredients. Here is her recipe for an extraordinary pie, handsomely wrapped in banana leaves.

SAGE'S TAMALE PIE *by Sage Conran*

SERVES 8

You will also need:

1 round pie dish 30cm/12in and 8cm/3in deep

1 round pie dish 30cm/12in and 8cm/3in deep

3 banana leaves, wiped clean (see tip, page 96); it is wise to have a fourth in case of mistakes)

FOR THE STOCK:

1 whole organic medium-sized chicken

1 bay leaf

1 tsp ground cumin

½ tsp ground cinnamon

8 sprigs fresh coriander

2 whole cloves

1 onion, peeled and halved

2 carrots, peeled and halved

3 ripe tomatoes, roughly chopped

1 tsp ancho chilli powder or regular chilli powder

This is a beautifully presented pie. It is hearty, but not as difficult as it may seem. It has a real Mexican flavour and can have a kick if desired. It is great for gatherings of family and friends, and is lovely served with a light salad.

Throw all the stock ingredients together in a large pan, then cover with H_2O and simmer for 1 hour. Meanwhile, butter your pie dish, take the pieces of string and lay them one at a time across the dish until it looks like you have drawn pizza slices with all the ends hanging over the side (pictured on page 97). Make sure the strings cross in the centre point of the dish.

Take two banana leaves and cut off any hard edges with scissors. Then run them lightly and carefully over an open gas flame or soak them in a sink of hot water. They will turn a beautiful bright green and become pliable enough to line your pie dish. Lay one leaf across the pie dish horizontally and one vertically, with the shiny side of each leaf uppermost. A few splits in the leaves are perfectly fine; just cover the dish as best you can, but you need to leave lots of extra leaf draped over the edges of your dish in order to fold it up and over the pie. Cut two circles from the third leaf, slightly smaller than the pie dish, and put aside.

For the filling, take the skin off the chorizo. Crumble it into a frying pan with the olive oil and fry over a medium heat, stirring, for 2 minutes. Remove from the heat and put to one side. Cut the mozzarella into 1cm (½in) slices and set aside.

3 cloves garlic, crushed

1 whole stick celery

1 whole red chilli

salt and freshly ground
   black pepper

FOR THE FILLING:

3 chorizo sausages

a splash of olive oil

300g (10oz) mozzarella
   (or more if you want it
   cheesier; you can use any
   cheese you want)

1 black olive

2 tbsp coarsely chopped
   fresh coriander

1 red chilli, deseeded and
   finely chopped (see tip,
   page 96)

FOR THE GRAVY:

2 tbsp masa flour or instannt
   polenta (see tip, page 96)

2 tsp cornflour

2 tbsp cold water

ingredients continued

Preheat the oven to 220°C (425°F/Gas 7). Meanwhile, make the gravy. First strain the cooked stock, retaining the liquid and chicken but discarding the other ingredients. Keep the chicken covered and leave to cool. Pour 850ml (1½ pints) of your stock into a pot and place it over a medium heat. Stir in the 2 tablespoons of masa flour and let it simmer for about 10 minutes. In a cup, mix the cornflour with the cold water until smooth and pour into the stock, whisking until you have a thickish gravy. When the gravy is cool, use a handheld blender to achieve a smooth finish. Put the gravy to one side. Taste and if it is a bit bland stir in a tablespoon of tomato purée and a teaspoon of vegetable bouillon powder. The chicken should have cooled by now, so strip the meat, roughly tear it and set aside.

To make the masa paste, combine the masa flour and salt in a bowl. Place the lard in a large jug and pour over the boiling water. Slowly add the hot water and melted lard to the masa flour a little at a time, mixing with a fork until you have a smooth paste. It should resemble a thick porridge; you may find you need more or less water. Spread half the masa dough in the bottom of the pie dish and press it flat with your hands, then layer on the chicken, chorizo and mozzarella. Pour over the gravy. Add the black olive anywhere randomly; whoever gets the slice with the olive in it has good luck, just like a sixpence in a traditional Christmas pudding. Fun for kids!

recipe continued

SAGE'S TAMALE PIE (CONTINUED)

1 tbsp tomato purée
  (optional)
1 tsp vegetable bouillon
  powder (optional)

FOR THE MASA PASTE:
450g (1lb) masa flour or
  instant polenta
1 tsp salt
70g (2½oz) lard or 5 tbsp
  olive oil
1.25 litres (2¼ pints) boiling
  water

TO SERVE:
1 handful fresh coriander
  leaves, coarsely chopped
8 lime slices

Sprinkle the pie with the coriander and chopped chilli. Cover it with the remaining masa and press flat with your hands. Cover with one of the leaf circles, shiny-side up. Fold the draped leaves up and over and trim them with scissors. Put the second leaf circle shiny-side up on top of the pie for a clean finish. Pull all the strings together, tie them in the middle and trim. Cover with foil.

Place the pie dish in a large roasting pan. Pour boiling water carefully into the pan until it comes halfway up the side of the pie dish. Cook the pie in the oven for 1 hour or until it has a nice firm top but has not dried out.

Serve with an interesting light salad and a glass of chilled light white, maybe Pino, or a fresh lime margarita with virgin strawberry margaritas for the kids. Just before serving, sprinkle coriander over each plate and add a slice of lime.

Tips – Chillies to taste: For a spicier pie, just add more chillies. My favourite ones are habeñero (Scotch bonnet), which get straight to the point.

Masa flour: Masa flour, or masa harina, is a Mexican staple used in many dishes including tortillas. It is made from crushed corn. Polenta is the closest substitute, though it tastes slightly different. If using polenta, replace the lard with butter, and follow the cooking instructions on the polenta packet.

Finding banana leaves: Cooking food in banana leaves is a very old technique. You can get them cheaply in Asian supermarkets. Alternatively, butter your pie dish, layer in the ingredients and simply cover with foil.

This is a wonderful winter pie, rich and luxurious. It's at its best when eaten by candlelight on a long, cold night with friends and plenty of good red wine.

PHEASANT & CRANBERRY PIE WITH PARSNIP MASH

SERVES 6

FOR THE FILLING:

500ml (18fl oz) good-quality fresh chicken or beef stock

1kg (2lb 4oz) pheasant meat, cut into 4cm (1½in) cubes

3 tbsp plain flour, seasoned with salt and pepper

2 tbsp olive oil

250g (9oz) bacon lardons

5 shallots, peeled and halved

2 cloves garlic, finely chopped

1 tsp crushed juniper berries

1 large glass red wine (about 300ml / 10fl oz), something chunky like Merlot or Shiraz

2 leeks, chopped

Reduce the stock by boiling it in a large saucepan for 30 minutes. Toss the meat in the seasoned flour until it is coated and set aside. Heat the oil in a large pot. Add the meat (in batches if necessary) and brown lightly for 2 to 3 minutes, stirring occasionally. Once browned, remove from the pan and set aside.

Put the bacon into the pan and fry until it is beginning to crisp. Reserve with the pheasant meat. Dump the shallots into the pan and fry them gently for 10 minutes, stirring them occasionally and checking that they do not brown.

Return the pheasant and bacon to the pan and set the heat to medium. Add the garlic and juniper berries, stir and heat through. Stir in the red wine, making sure you scrape up all the gubbins stuck to the bottom, and allow to bubble for 5 minutes. Add the leeks, stock and thyme and simmer for a further 30 minutes until the meat is tender, checking that it does not burn or stick to the pan and stirring occasionally.

1 tsp fresh thyme leaves,
  chopped

4 tbsp cranberry sauce

3 tbsp fresh flat leaf parsley,
  chopped

salt and freshly ground
  black pepper

FOR THE PARSNIP MASH:

800g (1lb 12oz) Maris
  Piper potatoes, peeled
  and cubed

500g (1lb) parsnips,
  peeled and cubed

50g (2oz) butter

50ml (1¾fl oz) milk

Meanwhile, preheat the oven to 220°C (425°F/Gas 7) and make
the mash. Boil the potatoes and parsnips in plenty of salted boiling
water until they are soft when poked with a sharp knife. Drain well
and return them to the pan. Add the butter and milk and mash until
smooth. I use a mouli (pictured on page 105), which makes a great
lump-free mash. Season well.

Remove the pheasant mixture from the heat and stir in the cranberry
sauce and parsley. Season the mixture to taste with salt and freshly
ground pepper and pour it into a pie dish. Top the pheasant mixture
with large spoonfuls of the mash all over. Using the back of your
spoon, smooth it over until the meat is completely covered, then use a
fork to form the mash into rough peaks, which will become lovely and
brown with crispy bits. Bake uncovered for 25 minutes or until golden.

I like to serve the pie with braised red cabbage.

Although this looks long and complicated it is a simple assembly with spectacular results. It is my version of the famous Yorkshire Pye, which was made as a traditional Christmas gift.

CHRISTMAS DUCK & FIG PIE

SERVES 10

You will need a 20cm/8in round and 6.5cm/2½in deep springform tin

FOR THE HOT WATER CRUST:

225g (8oz) duck fat (see tip opposite)

200ml (7fl oz) water

675g (1lb 8oz) plain flour

1 tsp salt

1 egg and 1 extra egg yolk

1 tbsp caster sugar

FOR THE FILLING:

600g (1lb 5oz) duck confit (see tip opposite) (about ½ duck)

1 large handful fresh flat leaf parsley, chopped

1 large handful fresh mint leaves, chopped

100g (3½oz) walnuts, chopped

salt and freshly ground black pepper

First make the hot water crust by boiling the duck fat and water together in a saucepan. Pour the flour into the mixing bowl of a blender, sprinkle in the salt and whiz in the hot fat and water. Add the eggs and sugar, and whiz again until it clumps into a ball. Turn the dough out onto a floured board and knead until it becomes smooth. Cover the dough and leave it to rest for 20 to 30 minutes.

Preheat the oven to 220°C (425°F/Gas 7) and make the filling. Roughly chop the duck confit, discarding the bones and about half the skin. In a large bowl, mix the duck with the parsley, mint and walnuts, and season well with pepper.

In another bowl, mix the nutmeg, cinnamon, ginger, figs and slices of duck breast, and season with salt and pepper.

Trim the chicken livers of any sinew and yellow bits (which are really bitter). Cut the trimmed livers into large chunks, mix with the brandy and season with salt and pepper. Set aside.

Roll out two-thirds of the pastry on a floured board and use it to line the tin. Push the pastry into the corners using your fingers, leaving about 2cm (¾in) hanging over the top edge.

Layer in the meats, starting with the duck confit mixture. Press half the mixture into the bottom, followed by half the duck and figs, pressing it all down with the back of a spoon to make sure there are no air gaps. Pour in all the chicken livers, followed by the remaining confit and then finish with the rest of the duck and figs.

½ tsp ground nutmeg

½ tsp ground cinnamon

½ tsp ground ginger

25g (1oz) dried figs, chopped

4 large duck breasts, skin removed, cut into slices 1cm (½in) thick

400g (14oz) chicken livers

2 tbsp brandy

1 egg, beaten

FOR THE JELLIED STOCK:

100ml (3½fl oz) chicken stock (home-made or the best you can lay your mitts on)

½ sachet of gelatine salt

Roll out the rest of the pastry to make a lid, leaving a little pastry aside to use for decoration. Brush the edges of the pastry with water and cover the pie with the lid. Press the edge firmly with your thumb to seal, and trim the edges. Brush the top all over with a little of the beaten egg and add the pastry decorations. Brush the whole pie again with the egg. Cut two holes in the top at opposite sides and near the edge, big enough to insert the thin end of a funnel; you will be pouring the jellied stock into the holes later.

Place the pie in the oven and bake it for 20 minutes. Reduce the temperature of the oven to 110°C (225°F/Gas ¼). Cover the pie with foil and bake for a further 3 hours. When the pie is cooked, remove from the oven and allow to cool to room temperature.

Place the chicken stock in a small pan and bring to the boil. Take it off the heat and stir through the gelatine until completely dissolved. Season the stock to taste with salt. Then, using a little funnel, gradually pour the stock into the holes in the top of the pie until no more will go in. Chill for 24 hours.

I like to serve this pie cold with a selection of cheeses, baked potatoes, chutney and salad.

Tip: Duck confit is preserved duck in duck fat. You can buy it in tins or jars. You can use the fat from the jar in the pastry.

Fishy Pies

This pie makes the perfect big family lunch; just double the quantities for 8, and double again for 16. It is almost impossible to refuse seconds (or thirds) of this scrumptious, creamy, nurturing pie.

CLASSIC FISH PIE

SERVES 8 SPROGS OR 4 GROWN-UPS

FOR THE FILLING:

250g (9oz) skinless cod fillet

250g (9oz) skinless smoked haddock fillet

salt and freshly ground black pepper

25g (1oz) butter

1 heaped tbsp plain flour

300ml (10fl oz) milk

1 bay leaf

4 eggs

150ml (5fl oz) double cream

250g (9oz) large cooked peeled prawns

1 handful fresh flat leaf parsley leaves, chopped

ingredients continued

Preheat the oven to 220°C (425°F/Gas 7). Place each fish fillet onto large, separate pieces of foil. Season with salt and pepper and top with a little of the butter. Make a couple of neat little parcels with the foil and bake for 10 minutes. Don't worry if the fish doesn't looked cooked through; it cooks further in the pie.

Melt the remaining butter (about 15g/½oz) in a large pan on a low heat and stir in the flour. Allow it to bubble for a couple of minutes, then whisk in the milk until the flour has dissolved. Drop in the bay leaf and allow to simmer for 10 minutes. Whisk occasionally until you have a smooth, thickish sauce.

Meanwhile, put the eggs in a pan of cold water and bring to a rolling boil for 6 minutes. Remove from the heat and run the eggs under cold water. Peel and quarter the eggs, then put them aside.

Whisk the cream into the sauce and keep it bubbling for another 10 minutes. Stir in the prawns and heat through. Take the pan off the heat and chuck away the bay leaf. Add the fish and any of its cooking liquid, flaking the fish into large chunks and stirring them through. Throw in the parsley and eggs and gently stir round. Taste the mixture and season well.

recipe continued

FOR THE MASH:

4 largish Desirée potatoes,
  peeled and cubed

1 small wine glass milk
  (about 150ml / 5fl oz)

100g (3½oz) butter

Turn up the oven to 240°C (475°F/Gas 9). Then make the mash by boiling the potatoes in plenty of salted water until very soft when poked with a sharp knife. Drain and mash the spuds. I use a mouli (pictured on page 105), as it makes a lovely lump-free mash. Stir through the milk and butter; don't skimp on the milk as you want a fairly soft mash. Add salt to taste, but you may need more than you think.

Pour the fish mixture into a pie dish. Spoon the mash evenly over the top in big dollops, filling in the gaps with the back of the spoon. Take a fork and rough the surface of the mash into peaks. Bake for 30 minutes or until the top is crisp and golden.

I like to serve this pie with runner beans and carrots.

This divine pie is based on an American chowder. The bacon gives it a rounded, smoky flavour. Buy cod that comes from sustainable stocks. Other fish to use would be halibut, hake or haddock.

COD & BACON

SERVES 6

FOR THE FILLING:

800g (1lb 12oz) skinless cod fillet

a large knob of butter

freshly ground black pepper

150g (5oz) bacon lardons

2 small white onions, sliced

1 tbsp plain flour

6 splashes of Tabasco sauce

250ml (9fl oz) milk

150ml (5fl oz) double cream

1 handful fresh flat leaf parsley, chopped

FOR THE MASH:

4 largish Desirée potatoes, peeled and cubed

salt

1 small wine glass milk (about 150ml / 5fl oz)

100g (3½oz) butter

Preheat the oven to 220°C (425°F/Gas 7). Lay the fish in the centre of a piece of foil big enough in which to wrap it. Place a little of the butter on top and season with pepper. Scrunch the edges of the foil together to seal it into a parcel. Place on a baking tray and pop it in the oven. After 10 minutes, remove the fish, reserving any cooking liquid for the sauce. Flake the fish into large chunks and set aside.

Throw the bacon into a large casserole and cook, stirring, until it begins to brown and the fat runs out. Chuck in the onions and the remaining butter and season with plenty of pepper. Fry gently for 10 minutes. Sprinkle in the flour and stir through. Then splash in the Tabasco along with any cooking liquid from the fish, the milk and the cream. Keep stirring until you have a smooth sauce. Let it gently bubble for 10 minutes, then remove from the heat and gently stir in the parsley and the fish.

Now prepare the mash by boiling the cubed potatoes in plenty of salted water until they are very soft when poked with a sharp knife. Drain and mash; use a mouli (pictured on page 105) for a really smooth mash. Stir through the milk and butter. You may need a bit more or less milk but you want a fairly soft mash. Add salt to taste.

Pour the fish mixture into a pie dish. Top with the mash, then fill in any holes with the back of the spoon. Take a fork and rough the surface of the mash into small peaks. Pop it in the oven. Bake for 20 minutes or until golden.

I like to serve this pie with buttered cabbage.

The slightly aniseed flavour of fennel goes extremely well with fish. The fennel seeds on top add to the flavour and have a nice crunch. Serve with purple sprouting broccoli or asparagus spears.

SALMON & FENNEL

SERVES 4

500g (1lb) skinless salmon fillet

25g (1oz) butter

salt and freshly ground black pepper

150g (5oz) bacon lardons (optional substitute: 2 tbsp olive oil)

2 small white onions, sliced

4 small fennel bulbs, trimmed, halved and finely sliced

1 tbsp plain flour

6 splashes of Tabasco sauce

200ml (7fl oz) milk

150ml (5fl oz) double cream

1 handful fresh flat leaf parsley, chopped

juice of ½ lemon

175g (6oz) good-quality butter puff pastry

1 egg, beaten

1½ tsp fennel seeds

Preheat the oven to 220°C (425°F/Gas 7). Lay the fish in the centre of a piece of foil big enough to wrap it in, dollop a little of the butter on top and season with pepper. Seal into a parcel and place on a baking tray. Pop it into the oven and bake for 10 minutes (the fish will finish cooking in the pie). Break up the fish into large chunks and reserve any cooking liquid for the sauce. Set aside.

Throw the bacon lardons into a large casserole and fry until they begin to brown and the fat runs out. If you've not using the lardons, just fry the veg in the olive oil and butter.

Chuck in the onions, fennel and the rest of the butter. Season with plenty of pepper, and continue to fry gently for 10 minutes. Sprinkle in the flour and stir through. Splash the Tabasco, the cooking liquid from the fish, the milk and the cream into the casserole and stir quickly until you have a smooth sauce. Let it gently bubble for 10 minutes. Then stir in the parsley, lemon juice and the fish chunks, and season with salt and pepper. Spoon the fish mixture into a pie dish, and set it aside to cool slightly.

Meanwhile, roll out the pastry to a piece large enough to cover the pie dish. Brush the rim of the dish with a little of the beaten egg, and cover the pie with the pastry. Cut the pastry to size, putting aside any unused pastry. Press the rim with a fork to seal and brush the top with beaten egg. Roll out the unused pastry and cut into shapes to decorate the top. Cut a small hole in the top to let the steam escape and brush again with egg. Sprinkle the fennel seeds all over the top of the pie. Place it in the oven and bake for 20 minutes.

Get your little pirates to help with this one –
peeling eggs, mashing spuds, measuring and
weighing. It's all good fun for tiny chefs and they'll
think it tastes better if they made it themselves.

FISH PIE FOR LITTLE PIRATES

**SERVES 8 SPROGS OR
4 GROWN-UPS**

FOR THE FILLING:

300g (10oz) skinless
    smoked haddock fillet

300g (10oz) skinless cod
    fillet

1 bay leaf

450ml (16fl oz) milk,
    or enough to just
    cover the fish

4 large eggs

4 handfuls frozen peas

25g (1oz) butter

1 tbsp plain flour

1 handful fresh flat leaf
    parsley, chopped

salt

ingredients continued

Preheat the oven to 220°C (425°F/Gas 7). Place the fish in your
pie dish with the bay leaf and milk. Pop it in the oven. After 10
minutes, remove the fish from the oven and lift it out of the milk.
Reserve the milk and bay leaf. Break up the fish into large chunks
and set aside.

Put the eggs in a pan of water on a high heat, and bring it to a
rolling boil. Allow the eggs to boil for 2 minutes, then add the peas
and bring the pan back to the boil for a further 2 minutes. Strain
the peas and eggs, then run them under cold water. Put the fish and
peas in the pie dish, then peel and quarter the eggs lengthways and
add them to the dish as well.

Now melt the butter in a large saucepan on a lowish heat. Stir in the
flour and let it sizzle for a couple of minutes, but don't let it brown.
Whisk in the milk and bay leaf reserved from the fish. Let it gently
bubble away for about 15 minutes, beating with a whisk from time
to time. Stir in the parsley and season with salt. Allow the sauce to
cool slightly, remove the bay leaf, then pour it over the fish mixture.
Stir the sauce through carefully, taking care that the eggs and fish
don't break up.

recipe continued

FOR THE MASH:

4 largish Desirée potatoes, peeled and cubed

100g (3½oz) butter

1 small wine glass milk (about 150ml / 5fl oz)

To make the mash, boil the potatoes in plenty of salted water for about 15 minutes or until very tender when poked with a sharp knife. Drain well and mash them with the butter, milk and plenty of salt. I use a mouli (pictured on page 105), which makes a gorgeous lump-free mash. Cover the fish with the mash by spooning it on in large dollops all over the top. Fill in the holes by smoothing over the mash with the back of the spoon, then take a fork and rough the surface of the mash into small peaks. Place the pie in the oven and bake for 20 minutes or until golden on top.

I like to serve this with buttered carrots and runner beans.

Salsa verde sounds exotic but simply refers to any green sauce. This particular green sauce has a great tang from the capers and mint. The grated potatoes on top become crunchy and delicious.

COD WITH SALSA VERDE

SERVES 2

300g (10oz) skinless cod fillet

salt and freshly ground black pepper

a knob of butter

75g (2¾oz) capers, rinsed

1 large handful (about 25g/1oz) each fresh mint, parsley and coriander

4 anchovy fillets

2 cloves garlic, chopped

4 tbsp olive oil

2 eggs

2 medium waxy potatoes, peeled, boiled and cooled

Preheat the oven to 220°C (425°F/Gas 7). Put the cod on a large piece of foil. Season with salt and pepper and dollop on a bit of butter. Bring up the sides of the foil, roll them together and fold the ends over the top to make a little package. Place on a baking tray, pop it into the oven and bake for 15 minutes. Don't worry if it is slightly undercooked as it will continue to cook in the pie.

Meanwhile, put the capers, herbs, anchovies, garlic and half the olive oil into a blender and whiz into a smooth paste. Place the eggs into a small pan of cold water and bring to a rolling boil over a high heat. Remove the eggs after 6 minutes, run them under cold water, then peel and quarter.

Remove the fish from the oven. Set it aside to cool, pouring the cooking liquid from the fish into the green paste and stirring through. Once the fish has cooled, flake it into a smallish pie dish. Add the egg quarters to the dish and stir through the green sauce.

Grate the potatoes with a cheese grater, as you would cheese, into a bowl and add the rest of the oil. Season it with salt and pepper and mix it all together with your fingers. Put the potato mixture on top of the fish mixture, covering it completely. Place the pie in the oven and bake for 30 minutes or until the potato topping is crisp.

I like to serve this pie with boiled baby carrots and broad beans or baby leeks.

Halibut is a wonderful, firm, succulent white fish. Together with the spinach and other vegetables, it makes a fabulously light and tasty pie.

Halibut & Spinach

SERVES 4

600g (1lb 5 oz) skinless halibut fillet

salt and freshly ground black pepper

1 handful fresh oregano leaves, chopped

a large knob of butter

2 tbsp olive oil

1 onion, chopped

1 stick celery, chopped

1 carrot, peeled and chopped

1 medium potato, peeled and cut into little cubes

200g (7oz) baby spinach

a pinch of ground nutmeg

200ml (7fl oz) double cream

300g (10oz) good-quality butter puff pastry

1 egg, beaten

Preheat the oven to 220°C (425°F/Gas 7). Put the fish on a large piece of foil, season with salt and pepper and add a little of the oregano and butter on top. Bring the sides of the foil up and roll them together. Then fold up the ends so you have a nice little parcel. Place on a baking tray, pop it in the oven and bake for 10 minutes. It will be slightly undercooked, but don't worry because it will cook more in the pie.

Heat the oil and the rest of the butter in a large lidded pan. Gently fry the onion, celery, carrot, potato and the rest of the oregano for 20 minutes or until soft, stirring it now and again.

When the potatoes are soft enough to be squashed with the back of a spoon, add all the spinach to the pot and cover it with a lid. Check and stir every couple of minutes until the spinach has wilted completely. Give it a stir, scraping all the gubbins stuck to the bottom of the pan into the mixture. Season it with salt, pepper and nutmeg.

Spoon the spinach mixture into a blender, pour in the cream and whiz until you have a smooth sauce. Take the fish out of the foil parcel. Cut it into chunks and mix it with the sauce.

Fill a pie dish with the fish and spinach mixture, then set aside. Roll out the pastry large enough to cover the pie dish and cut it to size, putting aside any unused pastry. Brush the rim of the pie dish with a little of the beaten egg. Lay the pastry over the dish and seal with a fork. Decorate the top with the unused pastry cut into shapes. Cut a hole in the top to let the steam escape and brush with the egg.

Place the pie in the oven and bake for 20 minutes or until the top has risen and is golden. Serve with fine beans, chopped parsley and new potatoes tossed in butter.

Haddock and black pudding may seem like an odd combination but it is a match made in heaven, completely irresistible and exquisitely simple.

HADDOCK & BLACK PUDDING MINI TARTS

MAKES 6 LITTLE TARTS

You will need 6 x 12.5cm (5in) round non-stick tart tins

FOR THE FILLING:

450g (1lb) skinless smoked haddock fillet

a knob of butter

salt and freshly ground black pepper

150g (5oz) black pudding

a splash of olive oil

1 egg

2 egg yolks

150ml (5fl oz) double cream

1½ tsp fresh thyme leaves, chopped

FOR THE PASTRY:

50g (2oz) prepared suet, such as Atora

100g (3½oz) self-raising flour

a large pinch of salt

2 tbsp very cold water

Preheat the oven to 220°C (425°F/Gas 7). Lay the fish on a piece of foil big enough in which to wrap it. Dollop on the butter and a grind or two of black pepper. Make the foil into a parcel, place on a baking tray and bake in the oven for 10 minutes.

Cut the black pudding into thick slices. Fry them in a little olive oil for 5 minutes and then set aside. Mix the egg and egg yolks, cream and thyme leaves together in a bowl. Season with just a little salt and plenty of black pepper. Set aside.

Make the pastry by mixing all the ingredients together in a large bowl until you have a soft dough. Knead the dough for a couple of minutes until it becomes smooth and a little elastic. Divide the pastry into six and roll out each piece big enough to line the tart tins. Push the pastry into the edges and trim the excess. Bake the pastry cases in the oven for 5 minutes, then allow to cool.

Meanwhile, flake the fish and chop the black pudding into chunks, discarding the skin. Divide them evenly between the tarts. Then pour over the egg and cream mixture, place the tarts in the oven and bake for no more than 10 minutes.

Serve with a lovely crunchy salad.

A perfect pie for lunch in the garden, this is based on a sort of French pizza called "pissaladière". It is great served with lots of different salads, and it goes down especially well with a pint of Guinness.

CARAMELISED ONION, ANCHOVY & OLIVE

SERVES 6 AS PART OF A SUMMER LUNCH OR 4 AS A MAIN DISH

You will need a 22cm (8½in) round flan tin

2 tbsp olive oil

a large knob of butter

5 medium onions, sliced

1 tsp dried thyme

½ tsp dried sage, crushed

freshly ground black pepper

100g (3½oz) black olives, halved and pitted

2 tbsp soft dark brown sugar

2 tbsp sherry vinegar

6 anchovy fillets

200g (7oz) shortcrust pastry, made with 66g (2½oz) butter and 130g (4½oz) flour (see pages 14–15)

Heat the oil and butter in a large pan on a medium heat. Dump in the onions and herbs and give it a good grind of black pepper. Allow to stew gently for 40 minutes, stirring now and again. It should become a lovely, sweet, soft mass. Stir in the olives, sugar and vinegar, and allow the mixture to cook down for another 5 minutes. Preheat the oven to 220°C (425°F/Gas 7).

Butter the flan tin. Roll out the pastry so when it is laid over the flan tin it droops over the edges by about 3cm (1in). Spread the onion mixture onto the pastry shell so it makes an even layer over the base. Lay the anchovies end to end across the onions in three lines. Then fold the pastry edges in towards the centre, leaving a gap in the middle. Place in the oven and bake for 20 minutes.

This goes wonderfully with a tomato and mint salad, roasted red peppers, cucumber and dill salad, couscous, borlotti beans with tuna, French bean salad, you name it.

Tip: You can customise the toppings. If you don't like anchovies, swap them for something else. Try strips of roasted red pepper or Parma ham, or perhaps cheese or capers. Think of it as a pizza pie.

I love hake. It has a very clean, fresh flavour and works well with the mint and lemon. I got the idea for anchovy pastry from the excellent snacks that they used to serve at Claridge's bar. They were made with puff pastry and had anchovy fillets rolled into the layers.

HAKE WITH LEMON & MINT

SERVES 6 AS A STARTER OR LIGHT LUNCH

You will need 6 x 12.5cm (5in) round non-stick tart tins

4 anchovy fillets

375g (13oz) shortcrust pastry made with 125g (4oz) butter and 250g (9oz) flour (see pages 14–15)

2 eggs

rind of ½ unwaxed lemon, grated

100ml (3½fl oz) double cream

1 handful fresh mint leaves, chopped

salt

500g (1lb) skinless hake fillet

Preheat the oven to 220°C (425°F/Gas 7). Pound the anchovies to a paste with a pestle and mortar. Roll out the pastry and spread the anchovy paste over it. Fold the pastry over the anchovies and roll it again. Continue folding and rolling until the anchovies are well distributed.

Cut the pastry into six equal pieces. Roll out each piece so it is large enough to line a tart tin. Line each tin in this way and then prick the base of each with a fork. Allow the pastry to rest for 10 minutes, otherwise it will shrink when baked.

Meanwhile, make the filling. Beat the eggs, lemon rind, cream and mint leaves together, and season with salt. Cut the fish into 4cm (1½in) cubes. Drop the fish into the cream mixture and stir it through.

Trim the excess pastry from the edges using a sharp knife, cover with foil and bake in the oven for 10 minutes. Remove the foil and bake for a further 5 minutes to brown.

Allow the pastry to cool. Spoon the fish mixture into the tarts and place them in the oven. Bake them for a further 7 minutes.

I like to serve these with a salad of Little Gem lettuce with a lovely mustard vinaigrette.

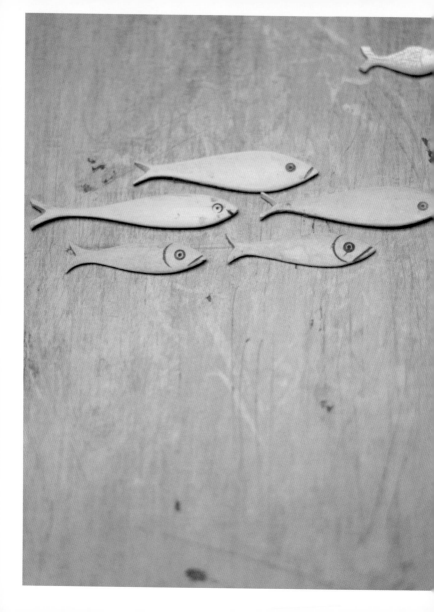

I made this pie for my daughter Coco one night when my son Felix, who hates fish, was out with a friend. It was a huge success.

QUICK FISH FOLDOVER

SERVES 3

500ml (18fl oz) fish stock

400g (14oz) skate wing (1 medium)

1 tbsp water

200g (7oz) baby spinach

2 tbsp double cream

1 tsp Worcestershire sauce

1 tbsp Dijon mustard

salt and freshly ground black pepper

375g (13oz) good-quality butter puff pastry

1 egg, beaten

Preheat the oven to 220°C (425°F/Gas 7). Bring the stock to a simmer in a large pan and poach the fish for 10 to 15 minutes until cooked through. Remove the fish from the liquid. When it is cool enough to handle, remove all the skin and bones and set aside.

Discard the stock and wash the pan. Return it to the heat with the tablespoon of water. Pile in the spinach and boil for 5 minutes, then remove it from the heat, strain and set aside.

In a large bowl, mix together the cream, Worcestershire sauce, mustard, salt and pepper. Squeeze as much liquid as possible out of the spinach and then chop it, add the spinach and fish to the cream mixture and mix it through.

Roll out the pastry on a large floured board and cut it into three equal rectangles. Plop one-third of the fish and spinach mixture onto one half of each pastry rectangle. Brush the beaten egg round the edges of the pastry. Close up the pastry case, as if you were shutting a book, by bringing the top flap over. Press down the edges with your thumb. Cut two diagonal slashes in the top of each parcel and brush them all over with the beaten egg. Place them on a greased baking tray and bake in the oven for 15 minutes until golden and risen.

Serve with buttered purple sprouting broccoli.

Make this pie if you are in a hurry. It can be thrown together and on the table in minutes. The almonds give it a superb, nutty crunch. An excellent light lunch.

SMOKED TROUT & ALMOND QUICK PIE

SERVES 2

50g (2oz) whole blanched almonds

salt and freshly ground black pepper

1 handful fresh dill, chopped

1 handful fresh flat leaf parsley, chopped

3 tbsp creamy goat's cheese

2 tbsp horseradish sauce

juice of ½ lemon

150g (5oz) smoked trout

2–4 sheets filo pastry

olive oil, for brushing the pastry

Preheat the oven to 220°C (425°F/Gas 7). Put the almonds in a dry frying pan on a medium heat. Sprinkle them with a little salt, and roll them around until they are slightly browned. They burn easily, so be careful. Set aside to cool.

Mix the herbs, goat's cheese, horseradish and lemon juice together in a smallish ovenproof dish. Season it to taste with plenty of pepper. Then flake the fish into the cheese mixture.

Crush the browned almonds slightly with a pestle and mortar, then gently stir them into the fish and cheese. Try not to break up the fish.

Brush one side of the filo pastry sheets with oil. Cover the top of the pie by lifting each piece of filo up in the centre and placing on top of the fish, to make little crumpled hills. Once covered all over, press the filo down slightly. Place it in the oven and bake for 15 minutes until crisp and golden.

I like to serve this with a lovely crunchy salad.

I was first served this dish by my kids' father.
I was so impressed. It was a fantastic colour and the
squid was wonderfully tender. It is also delicious
with polenta on top. (Do not eat it on a first date,
though, as it temporarily stains your teeth black!)

INKY SQUID PIE

SERVES 6

FOR THE FILLING:

a knob of butter

2 tbsp olive oil

2 large red onions, chopped

1kg (2lb 4oz) squid,
cleaned and cut into
1cm (½in) strips (see tip
page122)

4 cloves garlic, chopped

400g (14oz) tin plum
tomatoes

⅓ bottle heavy-duty red
wine, such as Merlot
or Shiraz

3 sachets squid or cuttlefish
ink (ask your fishmonger)

½ tube tomato purée

1 tbsp Dijon mustard

10 dashes of Tabasco sauce

1 tbsp redcurrant jelly

1 tsp herbes de Provence

salt and freshly ground
black pepper

ingredients continued

Heat the butter and oil in a large casserole. Dump in the onions and
gently fry for about 10 minutes til soft and sweet, stirring so they
don't burn.

Drop the squid into the pot and turn up the heat. Stir until the squid
has changed from translucent to opaque. Reduce the heat and stir
in the garlic. Let it fry for a minute before stirring in the rest of the
ingredients except the mash. Gently bubble your witches' brew for
1½ hours, stirring occasionally. Add a little water if it starts to dry
out; it should be a fairly sloppy consistency.

Preheat the oven to 220°C (425°F/Gas 7). To make the mash, boil
the potatoes in plenty of salted water until they are very tender when
poked with a sharp knife. Drain well and mash them with the butter,
milk and plenty of salt. I like to use a mouli (pictured on page 105)
to make a lovely lump-free mash.

recipe continued

INKY SQUID PIE (CONTINUED)

FOR THE MASH:

4 largish Desirée potatoes, peeled and cubed

100g (3½oz) butter

1 small wine glass milk (150ml / 5fl oz)

Put the squid mixture in a large pie dish. Cover it with the mash by spooning it on in large dollops all over the top. Fill in the holes by smoothing over the mash with the back of the spoon, then take a fork and rough the surface of the mash into small peaks. Place it in the oven and bake for 25 minutes.

I like to serve this rich, filling pie with a fresh, crispy salad.

Tip – Cleaning the squid: Pull the head away from the body. All the innards will slip out attached to the head. Cut between the eyes and tentacles. There is a crunchy bit between the tentacles, so make sure this is removed, but keep the tentacles. Slice down the length of the body and remove any gooey bits and the quill, which is a transparent backbone. Remove the membrane from both sides by scraping your knife over it several times. Cut the squid into strips about 1cm (½in) wide. If all this makes you feel squeamish, ask your fishmonger to do it for you, or buy raw squid rings.

This pie came from my love of fish stew, which combines fennel, tomato and saffron. The colours are fantastic.

FISH & FENNEL WITH SAFFRON MASH

SERVES 6

FOR THE FILLING:

75g (2¾oz) butter

300g (10oz) skinless salmon fillet

265g (9½oz) skinless haddock fillet

1 fennel bulb, trimmed and chopped into 1cm (½in) cubes, plus the frilly top

2 tbsp olive oil

1 onion, chopped

1 large clove garlic, finely chopped

1 large red chilli, finely sliced

salt and freshly ground black pepper

1 tsp tomato purée

ingredients continued

Preheat the oven to 220°C (425°F/Gas 7). Use a little of the butter to grease two large pieces of foil and place the salmon on one piece and the haddock on the other. Sprinkle the fennel tops over each. Draw together the edges of the foil to create parcels and place them on a baking tray. Bake in the oven for 10 minutes. The fish will still remain slightly raw in the middle.

Heat the oil and the rest of the butter in a large frying pan. Dump in the onion and fry until soft and translucent, being careful not to let it brown. Add the fennel cubes and fry for 15 minutes, stirring occasionally. Then add the garlic, chilli and salt and freshly ground pepper. Gently fry for a further 4 minutes. Stir in the tomato purée, and fry for another minute.

Pour in the tinned tomatoes and simmer for 20 minutes, stirring occasionally and adding a little water if it becomes dry. Remove the pan from the heat and add the fresh tomatoes. Set aside.

Once the mixture has cooled completely, stir in the herbs. Flake the fish into large chunks, and add it to the mixture. Stir it to combine but be careful not to break up the fish. Set it aside and make the mash.

recipe continued

400g (14oz) tin plum
  tomatoes

200g (7oz) firm plum
  tomatoes, such as pink
  jester, peeled and halved

1 handful fresh flat leaf
  parsley leaves, chopped

1 handful fresh tarragon
  leaves, chopped

FOR THE MASH:

300ml (10fl oz) milk

1 clove garlic, finely
  chopped

1 tsp saffron threads

900g (2lb) Maris Piper
  potatoes, peeled and
  cubed

100ml (3½fl oz) olive oil

Heat the milk with the garlic and saffron threads in a pan to almost boiling. Remove from the heat and set aside to infuse. Cook the potatoes in plenty of salted water for 15 to 20 minutes or until very tender when poked with a sharp knife. Drain well, return to the pan and mash them a little. Place the potatoes and the milk infusion in a bowl, and blend them using an electric whisk. Pour the oil into the mixture in a steady stream, whisking all the time, until all the oil is combined with the potato.

Place the fish mixture in a pie dish and top with the saffron mash, then take a fork and rough the surface of the mash to form small peaks. Place the pie in the oven and bake for 30 minutes.

I like to serve this with French beans, cooked then mixed through with a little butter and chopped garlic.

This is a mild and creamy pie packed with lots of fresh herbs. The smokiness of the fish goes nicely with the Little Gem, which also gives it a good crunch.

SMOKED HADDOCK & MUSHROOM WITH FRESH HERBS

SERVES 6

500g (1lb) smoked haddock fillet

1 bay leaf

½ tsp ground nutmeg

300ml (10fl oz) milk

50g (2oz) butter

2 tbsp plain flour

200ml (7fl oz) double cream

250g (9oz) button mushrooms, quartered

1 handful each fresh dill, coriander and parsley, chopped

1 Little Gem lettuce, quartered, cored and sliced

salt and freshly ground black pepper

375g (13oz) good-quality butter puff pastry

1 egg, beaten

Preheat the oven to 220°C (425°F/Gas 7). Place the fish, bay leaf, nutmeg and milk in a large pan. Allow to simmer for 5 minutes or until the fish is just cooked and flakes away from the skin easily.

Remove from the heat. Lift the fish from the milk and flake into your pie dish, discarding the skin and any bones. Keep the flakes quite large. Reserve the milk.

Rinse the pan and place it back on the heat, adding the butter and flour. Give it a stir and cook for a couple of minutes. Strain the milk into the pan, whisking until it becomes smooth and thick. Whisk in the cream. Stir in the button mushrooms and simmer the sauce gently for a further 15 minutes, stirring occasionally. Add more milk if the sauce gets too thick. Remove it from the heat, and stir through the herbs and lettuce. Season with salt and plenty of black pepper. Stir the sauce into the fish in the pie dish.

Roll out the pastry into a piece large enough to cover the pie dish. Brush the edges of the pie dish with a little of the beaten egg, and cover the dish with the pastry. Trim the pastry to size, keeping the unused pastry. Press around the edges using a fork to seal. Brush the pastry all over with a little more of the egg. Decorate the lid with pastry shapes cut from the leftover pastry. (I like little fish for this one.) Cut a small hole in the top to let the steam escape and brush the remaining beaten egg all over the decorations. Place in the oven and bake for 20 minutes or until golden.

I like to serve this pie with buttered French beans, peas and asparagus all mixed together.

Use a nice big piece of salmon for this pie. It is best to use a cut from the middle of the fish that does not include the tail, as it will cook more evenly. A small handful of chopped dill is a very tasty alternative to spinach.

SALMON EN CROÛTE

SERVE 6

200g (7oz) baby spinach

a pinch of ground nutmeg

salt and freshly ground black pepper

2 tbsp double cream

375g (13oz) good-quality butter puff pastry

500g (1lb) skinless salmon fillet

1 egg, beaten

Preheat the oven to 180°C (350°F/Gas 4). Put a tiny bit of water in a large lidded pot, just enough to cover the bottom. Put it on the heat so the water begins to boil, pile in the spinach and pop on the lid. Cook for 3 minutes, then strain it well in a sieve. Squeeze as much liquid out of the spinach as possible by using a spoon to press the spinach into the sieve. Set aside.

Rinse the pot and return it to the heat. Chop the spinach and plop it into the pot. Stir it around to dry it out further, and then sprinkle it with the nutmeg and season with salt and pepper. Take the pan off the heat and stir in the cream.

Now cut the pastry in half and roll out both pieces. They need to be big enough to sandwich the fish in the middle, leaving approximately 3cm (1in) around the edge for sealing.

Place your fish onto one of the pastry halves and brush the edges of the pastry with egg. Spread the spinach over the fillet and cover with the other piece of pastry. Gently press the pastry over the fish so it fits snugly.

Trim the edges to about 1cm (½in), and then press down with your thumb all along the edges to seal the fish into the pastry. Cut four diagonal slashes in the top to let out the steam, and brush the pastry all over with the egg.

Place the salmon en croûte in a non-stick roasting dish and bake it in the oven for 20 minutes. Serve with new potatoes tossed with chopped fresh dill, and baby French beans.

Veggie Pies

I like to make this tart in the summer. It has a very crisp, cheesy pastry and wonderfully sweet vegetables. The Roquefort is quite strong, so if you fancy it a bit milder, try something like smoked Gouda.

ROAST VEGETABLE WITH PARMESAN PASTRY

SERVES 6

You will need a large flat tin, approx. 20cm (8in) round

FOR THE PASTRY:

200g (7oz) plain flour

100g (3½oz) butter, straight from the fridge, cubed

100g (3½oz) grated Parmesan

1 egg

½ tbsp Dijon mustard

FOR THE FILLING:

1 red pepper, chopped into 3cm (1in) squares

300g (10oz) butternut squash, peeled, deseeded and chopped into 3cm (1in) squares

ingredients continued

First make the pastry by putting the flour and butter into a food processor. Blitz until you have what looks like breadcrumbs. Then add the Parmesan and give it a quick blast. Add the egg and mustard and whiz it until it forms a ball of dough. Wrap it in cling film and chill for at least 1 hour, but give it time to warm up to room temperature before you use it. The dough can be kept for 3 days in the fridge, or in the freezer for 3 months.

Preheat the oven to 240°C (475°F/Gas 9). Put all the vegetables for the filling into a baking tray with the herbs and oil. Season and then shake the tray to distribute the oil, herbs and seasoning evenly. Place the tray in the oven and bake for 40 minutes, flipping them over once after 20 minutes so they come out of the oven nicely roasted and evenly browned on all sides. When they are finished, remove from the oven and set aside. Turn the oven down to 200°C (400°F/Gas 6).

recipe continued

Roast Vegetable with Parmesan Pastry (continued)

1 parsnip, peeled and chopped into 3cm (1in) squares

1 sweet potato, peeled and chopped into 3cm (1in) squares

½ fennel bulb, timmed and chopped into bite-sized pieces

1 tsp dried rosemary, crushed

1 tsp dried thyme, crushed

2 tbsp olive oil

salt and freshly ground black pepper

100g (3½oz) Roquefort

Butter the flan tin. Roll out the pastry and line the tin with it. Prick the base with a fork and cover with foil. Bake it for 20 minutes and then remove from the oven. Place all the vegetables into the pastry base and crumble the Roquefort evenly over the top. Pop the pie back in the oven for 5 minutes or until the cheese is melted and oozing. When the pie is ready, remove it carefully from the tin and place it on a large plate.

I like to serve this with an endive and walnut salad.

I have tried to recreate a pie that I was served in India while on a trip with my aunty in 1981. It is a hybrid of English and Indian cooking. (We had pink blancmange for pudding, which was not nearly as tasty.)

ROASTED VEGETABLE WITH CUMIN PUFF PASTRY

SERVES 4

200g (7oz) each beetroot, parsnip, sweet potato and piece of butternut squash, peeled and chopped into 3cm (1in) cubes

3 tbsp olive oil

½ tsp garam masala

salt and freshly ground black pepper

200ml (7fl oz) tin coconut milk

3 eggs

125g (4oz) good-quality butter puff pastry

1 egg, beaten

1 tsp cumin seeds

Preheat the oven to 240°C (475°F/Gas 9). Plonk all the cubed vegetables in a large roasting tray, drizzle over the oil and season with the garam masala and salt and pepper. Place the tray in the oven and roast for 45 minutes, turning the veggies about halfway through.

When finished roasting, most of the vegetables should be mushy. Remove them from the oven and turn it down to 220°C (425°F/Gas 7). Stir the coconut milk into the vegetable mixture. It will look a bit like baby food, but the beetroot will still be in chunks. Set it aside.

Put the eggs in a saucepan of cold water on a high heat. Bring the water to a rolling boil and boil for 6 minutes. Run them under cold water, peel and cut the eggs into quarters. Place the eggs in the bottom of the pie dish, and spoon on the vegetables evenly. Set aside.

Roll out the pastry into a piece that is large enough to cover the pie. Brush the rim of the pie dish with a little of the beaten egg. Place the rolled pastry over the pie dish and trim to size. Press the pastry all around the rim using a fork to seal. Decorate the top of the pie with any unused pastry cut into shapes. Cut a small hole in the top to let the steam escape and brush the pastry all over with the beaten egg. Scatter the cumin seeds over the top. Place the pie in the oven and bake for 20 minutes.

I like to serve this pie with a lovely green salad.

I got the idea for this recipe from an Italian restaurant where I had delicious baked asparagus covered in mascarpone and Parmesan.

ASPARAGUS & QUAIL'S EGGS

SERVES 2

12 quail's eggs

150g (5oz) asparagus tips, cut into 2cm (¾in) pieces

50g (2oz) butter

10g (¼oz) plain flour, or about 1 tbsp

150ml (5fl oz) milk

150ml (5fl oz) double cream

½ tsp ground nutmeg

2 bay leaves

1 tsp Dijon mustard

salt and freshly ground black pepper

1 handful grated Parmesan

100g (3½oz) mascarpone or cream cheese

6 artichokes hearts in olive oil, drained and quartered

1 large handful fresh tarragon, chopped

2 sheets filo pastry

olive oil, for brushing the pastry

Preheat the oven to 200°C (400°F/Gas 6). Put the eggs in a pan of cold water and bring them to a rolling boil. Allow the eggs to boil for 2 minutes, remove them from the water and set aside. Put the asparagus in the boiling water and cook for about 5 minutes or until they start to lose their firmness. Strain and set aside.

Melt the butter in a large pan over a low heat. Add the flour and cook for a couple of minutes, but don't let it brown. Pour in the milk and cream and whisk until you have a smooth sauce. Stir in the nutmeg, bay leaves and mustard, and season with a little salt and plenty of pepper. Simmer gently for 15 minutes so it is just bubbling. Then stir through the cheeses, remove the bay leaves and set the sauce aside until needed.

Peel the quail's eggs and cut them in half. Mix the asparagus, artichokes, tarragon and eggs into the sauce and pour the mixture into a pie dish. Brush the sheets of filo on each side with olive oil. Cover the top of the pie by lifting up each piece of filo in the centre with your thumb and index finger. Place on top of the filling. Continue until the pie is covered with little crumpled hills. Once covered press the filo down slightly all over. Place the pie in the oven and bake it for 15 minutes. Cover with foil and cook for a further 10 minutes. The uneven top will be light, crisp and golden.

I like to serve this pie with a mixed green salad made with lots of chopped mint.

Springtime brings lots of lovely little tender green things. You can make this with any combination of fresh spring vegetables.

SPRING VEGETABLES WITH LEMON POLENTA

SERVES 4

FOR THE FILLING:

300g (10oz) courgettes, cut into 1cm (½in) slices

200g (7oz) asparagus tips and 175g (6oz) baby leeks, cut into 4cm (1½in) pieces

150g (5oz) peas, fresh or frozen

250g (9oz) broad beans, fresh or frozen

FOR THE SAUCE:

50g (2oz) butter

120g (4oz) leeks, finely sliced, white parts only

2 cloves garlic, sliced

180g (6½oz) Maris Piper potatoes, peeled and cut into 1cm (½in) cubes

100g (3½oz) fennel, sliced

150ml (5fl oz) dry white wine

ingredients continued

Bring a large pan of salted water to the boil. Add the courgettes, asparagus and baby leeks and simmer for 2 minutes before adding the peas. Bring everything back to the boil for a further minute and remove the vegetables from the water, reserving 250ml (9fl oz) of the cooking liquid. Run the vegetables under cold running water until they are completely cold. Drain well and set aside.

Bring a large pan of salted water to the boil, then reduce the heat and simmer the broad beans for 5 minutes. Run them under cold running water until they are completely cold, then set aside with the other vegetables.

To make the sauce, heat the butter in a large non-stick pan over a medium heat. Add the sliced leeks, garlic, potatoes and fennel and fry them gently for 15 minutes until all the vegetables are tender. Pour in the wine, turn up the heat and allow the mixture to bubble for 2 minutes. Add the cream and reduce for 1 minute before pouring in the reserved vegetable liquid. Simmer everything for 5 more minutes. Allow to cool. Then carefully pour the mixture into a blender and blend until smooth. Stir in the herbs, then the blanched vegetables. Pour the mixture into a pie dish and set aside. Preheat the oven to 220°C (425°F/Gas 7).

recipe continued

SPRING VEGETABLES WITH LEMON POLENTA (CONTINUED)

150ml (5fl oz) double cream
4 tbsp chopped fresh mint
4 tbsp chopped fresh parsley

FOR THE TOPPING:
500ml (18fl oz) milk
50g (2oz) butter
a pinch of salt
75g (2¾oz) instant polenta
rind of 1 unwaxed lemon, finely grated
1 large egg, beaten

To make the topping, warm the milk, butter and salt in a pan. When the butter begins to melt, stir in the polenta and heat until it is almost boiling. Stir continuously for 5 minutes and then remove it from the heat. Stir in the lemon rind and then the egg. By now the polenta should be soft enough to pour. If it is a bit thick, stir in a little more milk. Pour the polenta over the vegetables. Pop the pie in the oven and bake for 30 minutes until the top is golden brown.

I like to serve this with a Little Gem salad with sliced radishes.

Sometimes I get the kids to count how many fruits and vegetables they have had each day, and I am pleased to say it's usually much more than five. This pie has eight.

Tasty Tuscan Beans & Tomato Pie

SERVES 6

2 tbsp olive oil

a knob of butter

1 large onion, chopped

1 stick celery, chopped

1 carrot, peeled and chopped

½ tsp dried thyme

6 cloves garlic, chopped

1 small dried red chilli, crushed

salt and freshly ground black pepper

1 small glass white wine (about 150ml / 5fl oz)

6 tomatoes, peeled and chopped, or a 400g (14oz) tin plum tomatoes

Heat the oil and butter in a large pan over a medium heat. Dump in the onion, celery and carrot and fry gently for 10 minutes or until the onion is translucent, stirring occasionally so they don't burn or stick to the pan. Stir in the thyme, garlic and chilli, and season the mixture with plenty of black pepper.

Cook for 2 more minutes and then pour in the wine. Turn up the heat and let the mixture boil until the wine has evaporated. Reduce the heat again and add the tomatoes, tomato purée and parsley. Mash up the tomatoes a bit with your spoon. Let the mixture simmer for 10 minutes, stirring it occasionally. Then throw in the spinach and stir until it wilts. Add the beans and season with salt and pepper to taste. Cook for a further 10 minutes, then remove from the heat and set aside. Preheat the oven to 240°C (475°F/Gas 9).

Make the mash by putting the oil, rosemary and squash in a large roasting tin. Season with salt and pepper and mix through with your hands to coat the squash. Place it in the oven to roast for 15 minutes, then give the vegetables a stir. Roast for a further 15 minutes or until the squash is golden and very soft, then set aside.

½ tube tomato purée

1 handful fresh flat leaf parsley, chopped

200g (7oz) spinach

400g (14oz) tin borlotti beans, drained

FOR THE MASH:

3 tbsp olive oil

½ tsp dried rosemary, crushed

500g (1lb) butternut squash, peeled, deseeded and cut into 4cm (1½in) cubes

500g (1lb) Desirée potatoes, peeled and cubed

100g (3½oz) butter

While the squash is roasting, boil the potatoes in plenty of salted water until soft when poked with a sharp knife. Drain the spuds and mash them together with the butter and roasted squash until smooth. I like to use a mouli (pictured on page 105) for a lump-free mash. Season to taste.

Spoon the tomato and vegetable mixture into a pie dish. Spoon the mash on top in dollops and fill in any holes with the back of your spoon, then take a fork and rough the surface of the mash into small peaks. Place the pie in the oven and bake it for 20 minutes until golden on top.

I like to serve this with purple sprouting broccoli, French beans or green salad.

This is a recipe from my exotic friend Sophie Tremlett. Although she is French-Algerian, she was born and grew up in Guadeloupe and has since lived in Venezuela, Mustique, Barbados, Australia, Los Angeles and New York. She now lives in Shepherd's Bush (much handier for visiting). Sophie has been eating this pie since she was tiny, as made by her Algerian granny. We have no idea why it is called La Coca …

"La Coca"
Algerian Red Pepper & Tomato
by Sophie Tremlett

SERVES 6

You will need a 28cm (11in) round flan tin

1kg (2lb 4oz) red peppers

2 tbsp olive oil

5 cloves garlic, sliced

2 x 400g (14oz) tins chopped plum tomatoes

1 tsp crushed dried chillies

1 tsp ground cinnamon

1 tsp salt

Preheat the oven to 220°C (425°F/Gas 7). Bake your red peppers in the oven for 45 minutes, then take them out, place in plastic bag and allow to cool. As soon as they are cool enough to handle, remove the skin, pips and stalks and cut the flesh into long, thin slices.

Heat the oil in a large pan and gently fry the garlic for 1 minute before adding the tomatoes, chillies, cinnamon and salt. Cook very slowly over a low heat until the liquid has reduced; this takes about 45 minutes. Add your peppers to the tomatoes and simmer on a low heat for another 20 minutes.

In the meantime, prepare your dough. Pour the grapeseed oil and water into a large bowl, then add the cumin followed by the flour, little by little, until you obtain a smooth dough. Knead on a floured board for 5 minutes. Divide the dough into two balls and roll each one a little larger than your flan dish.

Grease the inside of the flan dish with a little olive oil. Lay the first layer of dough into the base, then spread over the red pepper and

FOR THE DOUGH:

200ml (7fl oz) grapeseed oil

200ml (7fl oz) water

1 tsp ground cumin

450g (1lb) plain flour

1 egg yolk

tomato mix and top with the second disc of dough. Seal the pie by rolling the edges towards the centre, as if you were rolling a cigarette. It should look like a covered pizza.

In a little bowl, beat the egg yolk with a little water. Using a pastry brush, paint this mix on the top of your pie. With a knife, make a tiny little hole in the middle of your Coca Pie for the steam to escape and bake for 1 hour. Check after 20 minutes and if it looks like it is going to burn cover with foil for the rest of the cooking time.

Voila, c'est fini et c'est très bon. Serve with green salad and a smile!

These are fab snacks and can be made in an instant. They are loosely based on Greek street food and are best served straight from the oven.

CRISPY SPINACH & MINT CIGARS

MAKES 24 CIGARS

250g (9oz) feta (see tip)

200g (7oz) spinach

1 large handful each fresh dill, coriander and basil

2 large handfuls fresh mint

½ tsp ground nutmeg

1 egg

salt and freshly ground black pepper

200g (7oz) filo pastry, cut into 20 x 15cm (8 x 6in) rectangles

50g (2oz) melted butter, for brushing the pastry

Preheat the oven to 220°C (425°F/Gas 7). Put everything except the filo pastry and butter into a blender and whiz until it becomes a thick paste. Brush both sides of the filo pastry rectangles with the melted butter.

To make a cigar, plop a soup spoonful of the green paste onto the centre of one end of a filo rectangle. Roll it over a couple of times and then fold in the sides. Keep rolling the pastry until you have a cigar shape. Place it on a baking sheet covered with greaseproof paper. Repeat the process with the rest of the filo pastry rectangles. Place them in the oven and bake for 20 minutes or until they are golden.

These cigars are perfect as a starter with aubergine salad, houmous, tzatziki and pitta bread.

Tip: Barrel-aged feta is best, as it is creamier and less salty.

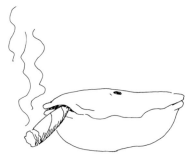

This is a gorgeous light pie with a fantastic crisp filo topping and is delicious hot or cold. The sweet squash and creamy goat's cheese are fantastic partners. This pie is very popular with my vegetarian friends. Try it with other roast vegetables or different cheeses.

BUTTERNUT SQUASH, SAGE & GOAT'S CHEESE

SERVES 6

800g (1lb 12oz) butternut squash, peeled, deseeded and cut into 3cm (1in) cubes

½ tsp crushed dried chillies

2 tsp cumin seeds

3 tbsp olive oil

sea salt and freshly ground black pepper

200g (7oz) firm goat's cheese, crumbled

2 tsp fresh sage leaves, finely chopped

1 handful walnut halves

1 handful fresh flat leaf parsley, roughly chopped

150g (5oz) filo pastry

50g (2oz) butter, melted, or 3 tbsp olive oil, for brushing the pastry

Preheat the oven to 180°C (350°F/Gas 4). Place the butternut squash pieces on a large non-stick baking tray. Sprinkle over the chillies and cumin seeds, and drizzle over the olive oil. Toss the squash to coat it well and season with sea salt and pepper. Place in the preheated oven and roast for 25 to 30 minutes or until the squash is just tender and starting to lightly brown. Then remove it from the oven and leave to cool.

Once the squash has cooled, place the squash in a large mixing bowl. Stir through the goat's cheese, sage, walnuts and parsley. Then spoon the butternut squash mixture into a pie dish and set it aside.

Brush the filo sheets on both sides with the melted butter or olive oil. Cover the top of the pie by lifting up each piece of filo in the centre with your thumb and index finger and placing it on the top of the filling, to make little crumpled hills. Press the filo down slightly. The uneven top will be light, crisp and golden when cooked. Place the pie in the oven and bake for 20 minutes or until the top is golden and the centre is piping hot.

I like to serve this with a cucumber and dill salad.

A fab summer pie packed with wonderful flavours, it is both light and filling. If you're feeding a crowd it's very easy to make this in a big batch using a large baking tray. It always goes down very well.

AUBERGINE, FETA & FILO

SERVES 4

4 tbsp olive oil

a knob of butter

3 red onions, chopped

400g (14oz) tin chopped plum tomatoes

2 tsp fresh thyme leaves, finely chopped

2 tsp fresh rosemary leaves, finely chopped

1 tsp ground cumin

2 tsp golden caster sugar

sea salt and freshly ground black pepper

3 cloves garlic, chopped

1 handful currants (optional)

1 large aubergine, cut into bite-sized pieces

1 handful fresh mint leaves, finely chopped

175g (6oz) good-quality feta, crumbled (see tip)

2 sheets filo pastry

a knob of butter, melted, or 2 tbsp olive oil, for brushing the pastry

Preheat the oven to 190°C (375°F/Gas 5). Heat 2 teaspoons of the olive oil and the knob of butter in a large frying pan. Stir in the onions and cook them over a gentle heat for 10 minutes until they are translucent. Add in the tomatoes, thyme, rosemary, cumin and sugar, and season well. Stew the mixture gently for 10 minutes, then stir in the garlic. Take the frying pan off the heat and stir through the currants, if using.

Heat the remaining oil in a clean pan. Add the aubergine and fry briskly, stirring continuously, until golden and thoroughly cooked. Next, stir in the onion and tomato mixture, the mint and feta. Pour it all into your pie dish and set aside.

Working quickly, brush the sheets of filo pastry with melted butter or olive oil. Cover the top of the pie by lifting up each piece of filo in the centre with your thumb and index finger and placing it on the top of the filling, to make little crumpled hills. Press the filo down slightly. Place the pie in the oven and bake it for 20 minutes or until golden. The uneven top will be light, crisp and golden once cooked.

I like to serve this pie with a crisp green salad and a yoghurt and cucumber salad.

Tip: I use barrel-aged feta, as it is creamier and not so salty. You could substitute a firm goat's cheese for the feta to vary the recipe.

One of my most magical food memories is of going on a gastronomic tour of Italy with my parents, which inspired the combination in this fantastically luxurious pie, filled with autumn's woodland bounty. The mushrooms are really meaty; a treat for vegetarians and meat-eaters alike.

CREAMY MUSHROOM & POLENTA

SERVES 6

FOR THE FILLING:

2 heads of garlic, separated but still in their skins

olive oil, for drizzling

10g (¼oz) dried porcini mushrooms

150g (5oz) unsalted butter

10 large shallots, finely chopped

1.2kg (2½lb) mixed fresh mushrooms, such as shiitake, chestnut, Portobello and button, all sliced

2 tbsp plain flour

100ml (3½fl oz) dry white wine

150ml (5fl oz) vegetable stock

Preheat the oven to 200°C (400°F/Gas 6). Place the garlic cloves on a non-stick baking sheet and drizzle lightly with olive oil. Pop in the preheated oven and roast for 15 to 20 minutes until the cloves are soft when squeezed. Place the garlic cloves in a plastic bag, twist the top to seal and allow to cool for 10 to 15 minutes. Remove the cloves from the bag, squeeze the garlic pulp out of the skins into a little bowl and set aside.

Meanwhile, put the porcini mushrooms in a small bowl and just cover with about 3 tablespoons of boiling water. Leave to soak for 15 to 20 minutes, then drain, reserving the liquid. Roughly chop the porcini and set aside.

Heat the butter in a large pan over a medium heat. Gently fry the shallots for 10 minutes until soft. Then stir in the reserved garlic and fry for 1 or 2 minutes. Add all the mushrooms, including the porcini. Turn up the heat and stir everything for 8 minutes or until the mushrooms have softened. Sprinkle in the flour and stir for 1 minute,

60ml (2fl oz) double cream

1 tsp Dijon mustard

2 tbsp fresh thyme leaves,
  chopped

salt and freshly ground
  black pepper

FOR THE TOPPING:

500ml (18fl oz) milk

50g (2oz) butter

a pinch of freshly grated
  nutmeg

a pinch of salt

75g (2¾oz) instant polenta

75g (2¾oz) Parmesan,
  finely grated

1 tsp fresh rosemary leaves,
  very finely chopped

1 large egg, lightly beaten

then pour in the reserved soaking liquid from the porcini, the wine and stock. Reduce the heat and let it simmer for 5 minutes for the liquid to reduce. Stir in the cream and mustard and cook for a couple of minutes before sprinkling in the chopped thyme. Season well with salt and pepper and remove from the heat. Once cooled, butter your pie dish and spoon in the mushroom mixture, then set aside.

To make the topping, warm the milk, butter, nutmeg and salt in a pan over a medium heat. When the butter begins to melt, stir in the polenta. Heat until it is almost boiling, stirring continuously for 5 minutes. Remove from the heat and stir in the cheese and the herbs, then the beaten egg. The mixture should be soft enough to pour. If it is too thick, beat in a little more milk.

Pour the golden polenta over the mushrooms. Place the pie in the oven and bake for 20 to 25 minutes until it is golden brown on top.

I like to serve this with buttered spinach.

These are great for a little snack or picnic in the park. You could also add chopped olives, anchovies or capers to the filling.

TOMATO & MOZZARELLA TRIANGLES

MAKES 15 TRIANGLES

300g (10oz) sweet ripe tomatoes, deseeded and chopped into little cubes

125g (4oz) mozzarella (drained weight), chopped into little cubes

1 handful basil leaves, chopped

½ tbsp olive oil, plus extra for brushing the pastry

salt and freshly ground black pepper

8 sheets filo pastry, cut into 10 x 25cm (4 x 10in) strips

Preheat the oven to 180°C (350°F/Gas 4). Mix the tomatoes, mozzarella, basil and olive oil in a bowl, and season with pepper. Add a pinch of salt to the mixture just before making your triangles, otherwise it will draw the juice out of the tomatoes and make it watery. Set the mixture aside.

Lay out the filo pastry and brush the top of the first strip with oil. Spoon a large dollop (you can use a soup spoon) of the tomato mixture at one corner of the strip. It is easiest if you place it at the bottom-right corner, when the strip is in front of you. Turn over the corner towards the long edge. The mixture is now under a triangle. Continue folding until you have a little triangular parcel.

Brush it all over with more oil and pop it onto a non-stick baking tray. Repeat the process until all the mixture and the filo sheets are used up. Place them in the oven and bake for 15 minutes or until they are golden brown. Eat the triangles warm or cold.

This pie is made with braised endives and two of its favourite companions baked together. Use the endive also known as witloof or chicory, you will recognise it as it looks like a large white cigar.

ENDIVE, ROQUEFORT & WALNUT PIE

SERVES 2

You will need two 12 x 4cm (4¾ x 1½in) ovenproof ramekins (or see tip)

250ml (9fl oz) chicken stock

100g (3½oz) butter

10 endives, trimmed and cut in half

100g (3½oz) walnuts, halved

100g (3½oz) Roquefort, cubed

125g (4oz) shortcrust pastry, made with 40g (1½oz) butter and 80g (3oz) plain flour (see pages 14–15)

Pour the stock into a wide saucepan big enough to take the endives in one layer, set it over a medium heat and add the butter. When the butter has melted, add the endives and simmer. Turn them occasionally until the liquid has almost evaporated and they become soft and coated completely. Remove them from the pan and allow to cool before slicing them into bite-sized pieces.

Meanwhile, preheat the oven to 220°C (425°F/Gas 7). Roast the walnuts in the oven for 5 minutes. Then stir the Roquefort cubes into the endives, along with the roasted walnuts. Tip the mixture into the ramekins or pie dish.

Roll the pastry out into two squares big enough to cover the top of the ramekins or pie dish. Drape the pastry over the pie(s), leaving the edges hanging down. Cut a small hole in the top for the steam to escape. I cook them just like this, but if you feel like it you can finish them like any other shortcrust pastry-topped pie (i.e. trimmed, sealed and brushed with beaten egg).

Place in the oven. Bake for 15 minutes for ramekins, or 20 minutes for a large pie, or until golden.

I like to serve this with roast beetroot and mint salad.

Tip: I make this recipe in large ramekins but it works just as well in a pie dish. Whatever you decide to use, make sure the dish is filled to just below the rim, so the pastry does not sag.

These little buns are stuffed with wonderful spicy, oily peppers and olives. Add some Parma ham, salami or anchovies if you like. I used to get something similar at Justin de Blanc's fantastic deli on Walton Street in London, when I worked as a toy buyer at the Conran Shop.

COLOURED PEPPERS & OLIVE LUNCH BUNS

MAKES 8 BUNS

FOR THE STUFFING:

2 tbsp olive oil

a knob of butter

1 red onion, chopped

1 each red, yellow and orange peppers, cored, deseeded and cut into strips

salt and freshly ground black pepper

1 small dried red chilli, crushed

3 cloves garlic, roughly chopped

1 handful mixed olives, pitted

125g (4oz) mozzarella, cut into 8 discs

ingredients continued

First prepare the peppers by putting the olive oil and butter into a heavy-bottomed saucepan over a medium heat. Stir in the onion and gently fry it for about 10 minutes until it is translucent, stirring from time to time.

Dump the peppers into the onions, and season well with ground pepper and crushed chilli. Add the garlic to the pot, throw in the olives and gently cook the mixture until the peppers are soft. This will take about 1 hour, so stir the mixture from time to time, making sure the peppers are cooking evenly and are not sticking to the pan. Once cooked, season to your taste.

Make the dough while the peppers are cooking. Put all the dry ingredients in a large bowl, adding the salt last. Mix through the water, followed by the olive oil, until it binds. (This can be done in a food processor.) Turn the dough out onto a floured surface and knead it for 5 minutes. Pop it back into the bowl and cover with cling film. Leave it to rise in a warm place for 30 minutes or until it has doubled in size.

recipe continued

COLOURED PEPPERS & OLIVE LUNCH BUNS (CONTINUED)

FOR THE BREAD DOUGH:

500g (1lb) strong bread flour

1 tsp golden caster sugar

1 tsp quick yeast

1 tsp caraway seeds

½ tsp salt

300ml (10fl oz) hot, not boiling, water

½ tbsp olive oil

Once risen, knead the dough for another 5 minutes and then divide it into eight equal balls. Flatten the balls to form discs about 20cm (8in) in diameter. Put a slice of mozzarella into the middle of each disc, topped with a dollop of the pepper and olive mixture.

Gather the edges together at the top and squeeze them together to close firmly; it should now look like a wonton. Then flip it over and gently flatten to form a bun shape. Place it on an oiled baking sheet. Repeat the process with the remaining dough discs and then leave them all to rise once again for about 30 minutes.

Preheat your oven to 220°C (425°F/Gas 7). Place the parcels in the oven and bake them for 20 minutes until they are golden and sound hollow when tapped on the base. They are best eaten warm.

I give these to my kids as a snack or as part of a picnic lunch.

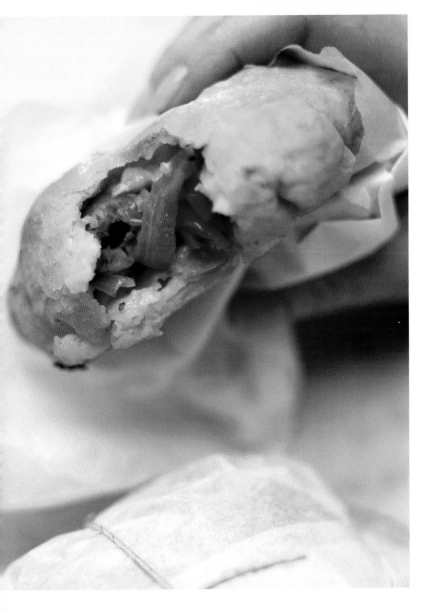

My daughter Coco has pronounced this pie as "the best, even better than the fish pies" (which she loves). The mozzarella melts and becomes very stringy. Quite a mess to serve but well worth it. Coco has even asked for it to be made on her birthday. Praise indeed.

STRINGY CHEESE PIE

SERVES 4 GROWN-UPS OR 6 KIDS

You will need a 22cm (8½in) round flan tin

2 tbsp olive oil

a large knob of butter

1 red onion, chopped

2 red peppers, cored, deseeded and sliced

salt and freshly ground black pepper

350g (12oz) tomatoes, peeled and chopped

300g (10oz) shortcrust pastry, made with 100g (3½oz) butter and 200g (7oz) plain flour (see pages 14–15)

1 handful basil leaves, chopped

250g (9oz) mozzarella (2 average-sized packets), sliced

Heat the oil and butter in a large pan on a medium heat. Bung in the onion and peppers. Season with freshly ground pepper, and gently stew for 15 minutes. Stir from time to time to prevent it from burning or sticking to the pan. Then stir the tomatoes into the peppers and season with salt and pepper. Let the mixture simmer for about 40 minutes until you have a thickish sauce. Remove from the heat and allow to cool.

Meanwhile, preheat the oven to 220°C (425°F/Gas 7). Butter and then line the flan tin with the pastry, keeping back enough to make the lattice top. Prick the pastry base all over with a fork and cover with foil. Pop it in the oven and bake for 20 minutes. When it has finished baking, remove it from the oven to cool.

Once the pepper mixture has cooled, stir in the basil. Spoon half the peppers into the pastry case and spread them evenly over the base. Cover with half the mozzarella slices, then repeat the process, finishing with mozzarella slices on top.

Roll out the remaining pastry and cut it into six long strips, about the width of your finger. Place three across the pie one way, followed by the other three in the other direction to make a lattice. Press the ends down and pop the pie in the oven for 20 minutes.

Check the pie after 10 minutes; if it looks like it might burn at the edges, cover it with foil.

This pie is great just on its own.

This is a bit like a glorified Welsh rarebit, and is just as tasty. It is yummy eaten hot or cold.

THREE CHEESE PICNIC PIE

SERVES 8

You will need a 27cm (11in) round flan tin

2 tbsp olive oil

a knob of butter

3 leeks, chopped

400g (14oz) shortcrust pastry, made with 125g (4oz) butter straight from the fridge, 275g (10oz) plain flour, 1 egg, beaten, and 50–100ml (1¾–3fl oz) cold water (see pages 14–15)

3 eggs and 1 extra egg yolk

50ml (1¾fl oz) double cream

½ tsp Worcestershire sauce

250g (9oz) goat's cheese, crumbled

250g (9oz) Roquefort, crumbled

300g (10oz) Emmental, grated

2 tsp Colman's mustard powder

salt and freshly ground black pepper

Preheat the oven to 220°C (425°F/Gas 7). Dollop the olive oil and the butter in a frying pan over a medium heat. Add the leeks and fry them gently for 10 minutes or until they are soft. Remove from the heat.

Butter the flan tin, and roll out half the pastry into a disc big enough to line it. Gently push it into the tin using your fingers. Prick the base all over with a fork about 15 times, and cover it with foil. Place it in the oven and bake for 15 minutes. Take off the foil and then bake the pastry for a further 5 minutes until it is golden. Remove it from the oven and allow to cool.

Meanwhile, beat the eggs, cream and Worcestershire sauce together in a bowl. Mix in all the cheeses, the leeks and mustard powder. Season the mixture with a little salt and plenty of pepper, then set it aside.

Roll out the rest of the pastry into a disc that is big enough to cover the pie. Pour the cheese mixture into the cooked pastry case, and cover with the raw pastry lid. Trim to fit, cut a small hole in the top to let the steam escape and place it in the oven to bake for 15 minutes. Then cover with foil and bake for a further 10 minutes. Allow the pie to cool before turning it out onto a plate.

I like to serve this pie with a rocket salad.

The sensational Antonio is my uncle and is married to my brilliant aunt, Priscilla. Antonio's jokes, like his food, are guaranteed to put a big smile on your face.

CALZONE DI SCAROLA *by Antonio Carluccio*

SERVES 6

You will need a pie tin 30cm (12in) round and approx. 5cm (2in) high

FOR THE PASTRY:

150g (5oz) butter at room temperature or 150ml (5fl oz) extra virgin olive oil

300g (10oz) plain flour

a pinch of salt

water to bind the dough

FOR THE FILLING:

the tender centres of 4 batavia heads (see tip)

salt and black pepper

100ml (3½fl oz) olive oil

2 cloves garlic, chopped

100g (3½oz) pitted olives

50g (2oz) salted capers, rinsed and dried

2 tbsp each pine kernels and raisins

1 small ripe tomato, seeded and cut into chunks

50g (2oz) anchovy fillets, cut into pieces (optional)

pinch of crushed dried chillies (optional)

Make the pastry by mixing all the ingredients together. Work into a ball, cover with foil or cling film and rest in the fridge for an hour. Meanwhile, preheat the oven to 180°C (350°F/Gas 4).

Boil the batavia in salted water for 5 minutes. Drain, squeeze the excess water out and cut into chunks. In a pan, heat the oil and fry the garlic, olives, capers, pine kernels and raisins until the garlic softens. Add the tomato and, after a few minutes, the batavia and anchovies (or you can omit the anchovies for a vegetarian pie). Leave for the flavours to combine for a while. Taste and season with salt, pepper and chilli, if desired.

Meanwhile, grease the pie tin. Roll the dough out with a rolling pin until it is about 3mm (⅛in) thick. Line the tin with most of the pastry, leaving some for the lid. Pile in the filling. Roll out the pastry for the lid, pierce with a fork to make holes to release the steam and place on top of the filling. Press the two edges of pastry together all the way round to seal, and bake in the oven for 50 minutes. This pie is delicious when served just lukewarm.

Tip: Batavia, known as scarole, also known as batavian endive or escarole, has sturdy leaves and a slightly bitter flavour. Young batavia leaves are tender enough to add to salads, otherwise batavia is best cooked as a side dish or used in soups and pies. Substitutes: curly endive (stronger flavour) or radicchio or rocket.

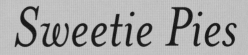

Sweetie Pies

Julian is a very talented food stylist, whom I have worked with for years. He baked all the pies for the pictures in this book, following my recipes carefully. I was very flattered that such an expert should be so complimentary. He cooked more than 10 pies a day. What a star.

LEMON MERINGUE PIE
by Julian Biggs

SERVES 10

You will need a 22cm (8½in) tart ring

FOR THE PASTRY:

250g (9oz) sweet shortcrust pastry, made with 75g (2¾oz) butter straight from the fridge, 25g (1oz) caster sugar, 150g (5oz) plain flour, a pinch of salt and enough chilled water to bind (see page 15)

1 egg yolk, beaten

FOR THE FILLING:

45g (1½oz) cornflour

1 tbsp cold water

juice and rind of 2 large unwaxed lemons, finely grated

ingredients continued

Preheat the oven to 180°C (350°F/Gas 4). Roll out the pastry and line the tart ring. Prick and blind bake, using dried beans (see page 13) for 15 minutes. Remove the beans and brush the pastry with the beaten egg yolk.

For the filling, mix together the cornflour, cold water and lemon juice and rind. Stir in the boiling water until it is smooth and transfer the mix to a pan. Simmer over a medium heat until thick: about 3 to 4 minutes.

Beat together the sugar and egg yolks with an electric whisk until pale and creamy. Then, whilst beating, slowly pour in the lemon mixture until thoroughly combined. Pour into the tart case and allow to cool and set.

recipe continued

300ml (10fl oz) boiling water

90g (3oz) caster sugar

4 egg yolks, lightly beaten

FOR THE MERINGUE:

4 medium egg whites

250g (9oz) caster sugar

Preheat the oven to 220°C (425°F/Gas 7). Meanwhile for the meringue, using an electric whisk, whisk the egg whites until they form stiff peaks. Continue whisking and slowly pour in the sugar until combined. Don't go too fast or the meringue will collapse; the slower the better. Once all the sugar is mixed in, use a palette knife or spatula to spread the meringue over the top of the tart, then bake for 15 minutes.

Serve with fresh cream and a few raspberries, if you like.

These are very simple little pies. You could use a good-quality lemon curd to make them even easier. I have used raspberries, but mango goes exceptionally well with lime if you are in a tropical mood. The lime curd is also wonderful on toast or drizzled over ice cream.

LITTLE LIME CURD & RASPBERRY PIES

MAKES 6 LITTLE PIES

You will need a non-stick 6-cup muffin tray

FOR THE LIME CURD:

4 egg yolks

6 tbsp golden caster sugar

juice of 6 limes

50g (2oz) unsalted butter, cut into cubes

FOR THE PIE CRUST:

300g (10oz) good-quality butter puff pastry

1 punnet or 150g (5oz) raspberries

First make the lime curd. In a small non-stick pan, mix the egg yolks, sugar and lime juice together. Place the pan on a medium heat and stir. Once it is warm, stir in the butter. It should mix in fairly quickly. Keep stirring until the mixture takes on the consistency of thick custard. Strain through a sieve into a bowl. Place it in the fridge and allow to cool for at least 4 hours.

Preheat the oven to 220°C (425°F/Gas 7). Butter the muffin tray. Roll out the pastry to a thickness of about 3mm/⅛ in. Cut the pastry into six rounds using a small upturned bowl as a guide. Line the muffin tray with the pastry discs.

Cover the muffin tray with foil, place it in the oven and bake it for 15 minutes. Remove the tray from the oven and take the foil off. The pastry will have puffed up completely and turned into something that looks like a Yorkshire pudding. Return the tray to the oven for about 5 minutes to brown the tops.

Allow the pastry to cool before carefully cutting off the tops. Take the pastry cases out of the muffin tray and hollow them out. Spoon the lime curd into each pie case, top with the raspberries and replace the pastry top.

I like to serve these with fresh cream or ice cream.

Lovely as a teatime treat or fancy-looking pudding, these pretty little treats are light and fruity, and easy as pie.

BLUEBERRY & STRAWBERRY FILO PIES

MAKES 12 LITTLE PIES

You will need a non-stick 12-cup muffin tray

100g (3½oz) melted butter

6 large sheets filo pastry, cut in half

icing sugar, for dusting

150ml (5fl oz) double cream

1 tsp caster sugar

½ tsp vanilla extract

12 large strawberries, sliced

36 blueberries

1 tbsp golden syrup

Preheat the oven to 220°C (425°F/Gas 7).

Butter the muffin tray. Brush each of the cut filo sheets on both sides with melted butter. Line each cup in the muffin tray with a filo sheet.

Put the muffin tray in the oven and bake for 5 minutes or until the pastry is golden. Remove the tray from the oven and set aside. When the pastry is cool, carefully remove the filo cases from the muffin tray. Dust them with icing sugar by putting some icing sugar into a tea strainer or sieve and then shaking it over the top of the filo cases.

Whisk the cream with the caster sugar and vanilla extract until it is thick, using an electric whisk. Dollop a spoonful of cream into each filo case. Pop a few strawberry slices and a few blueberries on top of the cream. Drizzle a little golden syrup over the top.

Super easy. This is my version of a traditional American apple pie.

APPLE PIE

SERVES 4

You will need a 22cm (8½in) round flan tin

75g (2¾oz) butter

6 Royal Gala apples, peeled, cored and quartered

100g (3½oz) golden caster sugar

1 tsp ground cinnamon

300g (10oz) sweet shortcrust pastry, made with 200g (7oz) fine white plain flour, 100g (3½oz) slightly salted butter, 100g (3½oz) golden caster sugar and 4 egg yolks (see page 15)

Melt the butter in a large pan over a medium heat. Stir in the apples, sugar and cinnamon. Let them simmer gently for 20 minutes, stirring them now and again.

Preheat the oven to 220°C (425°F/Gas 7). Butter the flan tin and roll out the pastry so that when it is laid in the tin it drops over the edges by about 3cm (1in). Press the pastry gently into the tin, leaving the edges flopping over the sides.

Pour the simmered apples into the pastry. Flip the edges of the pastry towards the centre. Place the pie in the oven and bake for 15 minutes.

Serve it warm with custard.

This is a bastardisation of the famous Tart Tatin. I usually find it so sweet my teeth ache, so I have reduced the sugar and added orange rind and ginger to cut the sweetness. This makes it wonderfully marmaladey.

APPLE, ORANGE & GINGER UPSIDE-DOWN PIE

SERVES 6

You will need a flat-bottomed cake tin, approx. 22cm (8½in) round; an ovenproof frying pan also works well

4 eating apples

125g (4oz) butter

100g (3½oz) golden caster sugar

rind of 1 unwaxed orange, finely grated

50g (2oz) crystallised ginger, chopped

300g (10oz) good-quality butter puff pastry

Peel the apples, then cut them in half, end to end, removing the core with a small knife. Put the butter, sugar and grated orange rind into the cake tin, place on the hob and gently simmer until the sugar has completely dissolved.

Add the apples, round-side down, cover and let it bubble away for 30 minutes, checking occasionally to make sure it has not burnt, though a little burning is fine, as it adds to the caramel. Meanwhile, preheat the oven to 200°C (400°F/Gas 6).

Take the apples off the heat and sprinkle the ginger over the top. Roll out the pastry to cover the top of the apples, trim to fit and place in the oven for 15 minutes or until the pastry is cooked and golden.

Allow to cool a little before turning the pie onto a plate. To do this, put a plate over the tin and quickly flip it over so the pastry is on the bottom.

Serve with crème fraîche.

This is so easy and wonderful for a big family get-together. It takes moments to assemble and milliseconds to be gobbled up.

EASY PEASY PLUM & BLACKBERRY

SERVES 6

You will need a 24cm (9½in) round flan tin

375g (13oz) vanilla or plain sweet shortcrust pastry made with 125g (4oz) butter and 250g (9oz) plain flour (see page 15)

150g (5oz) blackberries

4 large plums, stoned and thinly sliced

2 tbsp golden caster sugar

Preheat the oven to 220°C (425°F/Gas 7).

Butter the flan tin. Roll out the pastry so it is a bit larger than the tin. Line the tin with the pastry, leaving some hanging over the edge. Pile the fruit into the pastry, and sprinkle it with half the sugar. Fold the rough pastry edges over the fruit (there should be a big gap in the middle) and sprinkle over the rest of the sugar.

Place the pie in the oven and bake for 20 minutes. Cover with foil and then bake for another 15 minutes.

Serve with cream.

Mark heads up the restaurant teams at the Bluebird, on the King's Road in London. Mark's forte is British food; he has been delighting the nation's taste buds with his talents for years.

MARK'S FAMOUS APPLE CRUMBLE
by Mark Broadbent

SERVES 6

6 large Bramley apples, peeled, cored and diced

225g (8oz) unsalted butter

soft light brown sugar, to taste

1 cinnamon stick

2 star anise

115g (4oz) plain flour

rind of ¼ unwaxed lemon, finely grated

rind of ¼ unwaxed orange, finely grated

55g (2oz) nibbed almonds

30g (1oz) ground almonds

55g (2oz) muscovado sugar

FOR THE CARAMELISED APPLES:

1 Bramley apple

140g (5oz) granulated sugar

300ml (10fl oz) water

Preheat the oven to 190°C (375°F/Gas 5). In a heavy-bottomed pan, sauté the apples in half the butter. Add the soft light brown sugar, cinnamon stick and star anise and cook for 10 to 15 minutes until the apples are caramelised and soft.

Make the crumble by putting the flour and remaining butter in a food processor and whizzing until the mixture resembles breadcrumbs. Alternatively, sift the flour into a large bowl and lightly rub in the remaining butter with your fingertips. Stir in the lemon and orange rind, nibbed and ground almonds and muscovado sugar.

Spread the crumble on a baking tray and cook in the oven for 10 minutes. Move it around with a fork. Put the sautéed apples in an ovenproof dish and cover with the crumble. Cook for 15 minutes in the preheated oven.

If you want to serve the crumble with caramelised apple slices, cut 8 to 12 very thin slices from the centre of the apple. Make a sugar syrup by heating the granulated sugar with the water until it has dissolved. Boil to a syrupy consistency. Dip each apple slice in the syrup, then set them on a wire rack somewhere warm to dry out a little. Put the slices under a medium grill and caramelise on each side.

Serve each portion of crumble with a couple of caramelised apple slices and cream or custard.

Tip: To make Blackberry and Apple Crumble, add 200g (7oz) of blackberries and take out some of the apples.

The finished fruit mixture used in this pie improves with age. It can be kept for ages if stored in the fridge in an airtight container, so it makes a wonderful stand-by pudding.

WINTER SPICED FRUIT PIE

SERVES 6

100g (3½oz) each dried apricots, prunes and dried figs, roughly chopped

50g (2oz) dried cranberries

½ tsp ground mixed spice

2 Earl Grey tea bags

100ml (3½fl oz) cranberry or orange juice

2 tbsp demerara sugar

50g (2oz) crystallised ginger, finely chopped

300g (10oz) good-quality butter puff pastry

1 egg, beaten

Put the fruit, mixed spice and tea bags in a large bowl. Cover with boiling water and leave it all to infuse for 10 minutes. Remove the tea bags and let the mixture stand overnight or for a minimum of 6 hours.

Preheat the oven to 220°C (425°F/Gas 7). Strain the liquid from the fruit into a saucepan. Then add the cranberry or orange juice, sugar and ginger to the pan. Place the pan on the heat and boil for about 10 minutes or until the liquid becomes syrupy. Add the fruit to the mixture and heat it through for about 5 minutes.

Fill a pie dish with the fruit mixture and set it aside. Roll out the pastry so it is large enough to cover the pie. Brush the rim of the pie dish with a little of the beaten egg. Place the pastry over the pie dish and trim it to size. Press all around the rim with a fork to seal it, putting aside any unused pastry.

Decorate the top with the unused pastry cut into shapes. Brush the top of the pie all over with the beaten egg. Place it in the oven and bake for 20 minutes or until the top is golden.

Serve with double cream (or Jersey if you can find it) or ice cream.

The mince pie first appeared in the Middle Ages and, yes, they contained minced meat, usually mutton. They also contained cinnamon, nutmeg and cloves, spices brought back by the Crusaders on their return from the Holy Land. Mince pies were known as Christmas pye because these exotic flavourings represented the gifts offered to the Christ child by the Three Kings.

MINCE PIES

MAKES 24 MINI MINCE PIES

You will need two 12-cup mini muffin trays

FOR THE ROSE PASTRY:

100g (3½oz) unsalted butter, straight from the fridge

150g (5oz) plain flour

a pinch of salt

1 tbsp caster sugar

1 tbsp rosewater

½–1 tbsp chilled water

FOR THE FILLING:

200g (7oz) jar good-quality mincemeat

1 tbsp icing sugar

This pastry is best made the day before. Cut the butter into cubes, and put it into a food processor with the flour and salt. Using the cutting blade, blitz until it resembles fine breadcrumbs. Add the sugar and pulse it until mixed in. Add the rosewater and the chilled water, a little at a time. Pulse the mixture until it binds together into a ball. Scoop it out of the food processor and dust with flour. Form the dough into a thick disc. Cover with cling film and chill for an hour in the fridge. Allow the pastry to come back to room temperature before using.

Butter the two mini muffin trays and preheat the oven to 220°C (425°F/Gas 7). Roll out the pastry on a floured board, dusting your rolling pin with flour too. Roll it as thin as you can. Cut into 24 discs using an upturned glass or biscuit cutter with a diameter of about 6½cm (2½in). Push the pastry discs into the muffin cups. Scoop about half a teaspoon of mincemeat into each cup. Cut little tops for the tarts from the remaining dough in the shape of stars, hearts or the more traditional discs. Place a top on each of the pies.

Put the muffin trays in the oven and bake for 15 minutes, then remove from the oven and allow to cool slightly. Dust each one with icing sugar by putting the icing sugar into a tea strainer or sieve and gently shaking it over the pies.

This is essentially a chocolate cake sandwich. It is an American dish and I have only seen a photo, so this may be completely wrong. But I could not resist having a go at a pie called "whoopie" and it tastes great too. It's perfect for kids' parties if you like hearing whoops of delight!

WHOOPIE PIE

**MAKES 2 PIES;
EACH SERVES 4**

100g (3½oz) bar milk chocolate

150g (5oz) soft butter

75g (2¾oz) golden caster sugar

1 tbsp cocoa powder, plus extra for dusting

1 tsp vanilla extract

4 eggs, separated

100g (3½oz) self-raising flour

ingredients continued

Preheat the oven to 110°C (225°F/Gas ¼). Break up the chocolate onto a plate, and pop it in the oven to melt for 15 minutes. Remove the chocolate and turn the oven up to 220°C (425°F/Gas 7). Set the chocolate aside.

Using an electric whisk, cream the butter and sugar together for about 3 minutes until it becomes pale. Beat in the cocoa powder and vanilla extract, and then the egg yolks followed by the melted chocolate. Lastly, quickly beat in the flour. Set the mixture aside.

Clean the whisk and then whisk the egg whites in a bowl until they are stiff. Using a large metal spoon, slowly fold two large spoonfuls of the egg whites into the chocolate mixture. Carefully fold in the rest of the egg whites, trying to keep them as fluffy as possible. Don't be tempted to over-mix, as you will lose the air.

Line two large baking sheets with foil. Plop the chocolate mixture in four large round dollops onto the foil, two on each baking sheet. Don't put them too close together, as they will expand. They will look a bit like little cow pats at this stage.

Place them in the oven. After 10 minutes, cover with foil and bake for a further 10 minutes. Leave to cool.

recipe continued

WHOOPIE PIE (CONTINUED)

FOR THE FILLING:

284 ml (10fl oz) double cream (1 medium pot)

1 tbsp golden caster sugar

1 tsp vanilla extract

2 handfuls blueberries

2 handfuls blackberries or raspberries

Meanwhile, make the filling by whisking the cream with the sugar and vanilla extract until it is fairly stiff. Once all your cakes have cooled, remove them from the foil by wiggling a metal spatula underneath them. Put aside until needed.

Spoon the filling onto the flat side of two of the cakes. Scatter with the fruit and then cover each with the remaining cakes. Dust the top of the pies by putting cocoa powder in a tea strainer or sieve and shaking it over the top.

This is more of a caramel and pecan tart than a traditional pecan pie, but is exceedingly tasty. My mum was horrified when I gave her this unconventional version in the pub, but once she had tasted it she was a convert. This pie should be made the day before, as it needs to chill for 24 hours.

PECAN PIE

SERVES 12

You will need a tart tin approx. 25cm (10in) round

125g (4oz) pecan nuts

100g (3½oz) butter

250g (9oz) demerara sugar

375g (13oz) vanilla sweet shortcrust pastry made with 125g (4oz) butter and 250g (9oz) plain flour (see page 15)

200ml (7fl oz) double cream

1 tsp orange or vanilla extract

Preheat the oven to 220°C (425°F/Gas 7). Roast the nuts in the oven for 5 minutes. Melt the butter and sugar together in a small pan on a medium heat. Let it bubble for 20 minutes until the butter and sugar combine.

Meanwhile, roll out the pastry so it is large enough to line the buttered tart tin. Prick the base with a fork several times. Place it in the oven and bake for 15 minutes. Remove it and allow it to cool.

Once the sugar and butter are melted together, remove them from the heat and let them cool for 5 minutes or so. Then stir in the cream, orange or vanilla extract and roasted nuts. Pour the mixture into the pastry case and allow it to cool for a few minutes. Cover with cling film, then pop it in the fridge for 24 hours.

I like to serve this pie with vanilla ice cream or orange sorbet.

This was a bit of an experiment. The little guinea pigs all squealed the apricots were too sour; the big ones loved the tartness. You can use only apricots or only pears – in fact, you can use any soft fruit you have.

Pear & Apricot Tart

SERVES 6

You will need a tart tin approx. 27cm (11in) round

400g (14oz) sweet shortcrust pastry made with 180g (6½oz) butter and 100g (3½oz) plain flour (see page 15)

3 apricots, halved and stoned

3 pears, peeled, cored and cut into 8, end to end

2 eggs and 1 extra egg yolk

4 tbsp ground almonds

250ml (9fl oz) double cream

1 tsp vanilla extract

rind of 1 unwaxed orange, finely grated

2 tbsp caster sugar

Preheat the oven to 220°C (425°F/Gas 7). Butter the flan dish. Roll out the pastry and use it to line the dish. Place in the oven and bake for 15 minutes, then set aside to cool slightly.

Arrange the apricot halves like a flower in the middle of the pastry case. Arrange the pear pieces around the apricot like a fan, then set aside, while you prepare the custard.

In a bowl, mix the eggs and almonds to a paste. Add the cream, vanilla extract, orange rind and sugar, and mix thoroughly. Pour over the fruit.

Bake for 25 minutes or until the centre is only slightly wobbly.

Serve hot or cold with double cream.

Prunes with Armagnac is a time-honoured combination. The filling of this pie is creamy, and the crust is light and biscuity.

ARMAGNAC, PRUNE & GINGER LITTLE PIES

SERVES 6

You will need 6 small non-stick tart tins

FOR THE SWEET PASTRY:

200g (7oz) fine white plain flour

100g (3½oz) slightly salted butter

100g (3½oz) golden caster sugar

4 egg yolks

FOR THE FILLING:

200g (7oz) stoned prunes, chopped

150ml (5fl oz) Armagnac, Cognac or brandy

2 eggs and 1 extra egg yolk

250ml (9fl oz) double cream

1 tsp vanilla extract

rind of 1 unwaxed orange, finely grated

100g (3½oz) crystallised ginger, chopped

100g (3½oz) pistachio slivers or chopped

For the filling, soak the prunes in the Armagnac overnight.

To make the pastry, put the flour into a large bowl and rub the butter in between your thumb and fingers until it resembles breadcrumbs. Mix in the sugar and egg yolks to form a dough, then knead it lightly for 5 minutes. Wrap the pastry in cling film and put in the fridge for 1 hour, allowing it to come back to room temperature before using. This pastry is a bugger to work with, but it does have a lovely biscuity texture.

Preheat the oven to 200°C (400°F/Gas 6). Beat together the eggs, cream and vanilla extract, then stir in the orange rind, ginger, prunes and any excess Armagnac in a large bowl.

Roll out the pastry on a floured board until it is about 3mm (⅛in) thick and cut out circles big enough to line each tart tin (I use a small plate as a template). Prick the base with a fork. Bake for 10 minutes, cover with foil and return to the oven for a further 5 minutes. Allow to cool.

Pour the prune mixture into the pastry cases. Pop them back into the oven for a further 15 minutes.

Carefully remove the pies from the tins with a metal spatula. Sprinkle with pistachios and serve warm with cream.

Tip: It is possible to buy prunes already soaked in Armagnac, which would be just the ticket.

My daughter Coco hates raisins, so I have replaced them with dried apricots. The colour of the apricots and pistachios together are divine, and the subtle flavours of honey and cardamom bring an extra depth to the flavour. This delicious family favourite gets a lovely crusty top once baked.

CARDAMOM & HONEY BREAD & BUTTER PUDDING

SERVES 6

200ml (7fl oz) milk

200ml (7fl oz) double cream

6 cardamom pods, crushed

1 tsp vanilla extract

2 tbsp golden caster sugar

1 tbsp clear honey

enough butter to butter the bread

8 thick slices white bread, crusts removed

2 handfuls pistachio or almond slivers

2 handfuls dried apricots, chopped

2 eggs, beaten

Put the milk, cream, cardamom, vanilla extract, sugar and honey in a pan and heat to almost boiling, but do not boil. Stir until the sugar has dissolved, then set aside for 20 minutes to allow the flavours to infuse.

Butter the bread and grease an ovenproof dish big enough to take the bread slices in two layers. Lay the bread in the bottom of the dish and scatter with half the nuts and fruit. Cover with another layer of bread and fruit.

Preheat the oven to 220°C (425°F/Gas 7). Mix the eggs into the cream mixture and pour through a sieve over the bread, then gently press the bread down into the cream mixture so it soaks it up. Leave for 15 minutes for the bread to become fully saturated.

Bake in the oven for 25 minutes. Cover with foil after about 15 minutes so the fruit and nuts on top don't burn.

Serve with cream.

Ok, it's not really a pie, but it's just too good not to include. If you can make a basic sponge cake or fairy cake, this will be a doddle. It will also guarantee friendship for life from whomever you serve it to. It really is food of the gods.

STICKY TOFFEE PUDDING PIE

SERVES 10

You will need a 24cm (9½in) round springform tin

250g (9oz) stoned dates, chopped

300ml (10fl oz) water

walnut-sized piece of fresh ginger, peeled and grated

1 tsp vanilla extract

1 tsp bicarbonate of soda

100g (3½oz) soft butter

250g (9oz) golden caster sugar

3 eggs

350g (12½oz) self-raising flour

½ tsp baking powder

FOR THE TOFFEE SAUCE:

200g (7oz) butter

350g (12oz) soft dark brown sugar

300ml (10fl oz) double cream

Preheat the oven to 180°C (350°F/Gas 4). Put the dates, water, ginger and vanilla extract in a pan and bring to the boil. Take off the heat and leave to stand for 5 minutes before stirring in the bicarbonate of soda.

Using an electric whisk, cream the butter and sugar together until it becomes pale, add the eggs and then stir in the flour and baking powder. Fold in the date mixture. Pour into a well-greased springform tin and bake for 35 minutes or until when pricked with a skewer it comes out clean.

While the pudding is cooking, make the sauce. Mix the butter, sugar and cream together in a pan and boil for 5 minutes, then set aside. Allow the cake to cool, then poke a few holes in the top with a skewer, pour a little of the sauce over the cake and let it soak in.

Just before serving, spread a little sauce over the top of the cake and pop it back in the oven for 5 minutes at 180°C (350°F/Gas 4) to give it a crunchy top. Serve any extra sauce hot with the pudding.

I like to serve this with vanilla ice cream.

This is one of the easiest recipes I know and is really great for a big Sunday family lunch. It's also nice with a bit of cinnamon added into the crushed biscuits. You will need to make the biscuit base 24 hours ahead.

BANOFFEE PIE

SERVES 8

You will need a 24cm (9½in) round springform tin

18 digestive biscuits

200g (7oz) butter, melted

400g (14oz) tin condensed milk

4 bananas, thinly sliced

400ml (14fl oz) double cream

½ tsp vanilla extract

1 tbsp caster sugar

2 pieces of chocolate

Place the digestives in the tin. Crush them well using a potato masher or the end of a rolling pin. Pour the melted butter over the crushed biscuits and mix it well. Pat the biscuit mixture down until it is compact and flat, and then place the tin in the fridge to let the base harden overnight.

Put the unopened tin of condensed milk in a pan and cover with a lid. Fill the pan with water so it comes halfway up the tin. Simmer over a low heat for 2½ hours, topping up the water as necessary. Remove the tin from the pan and run cold water over it until it is completely cool. Set aside.

Remove the biscuit base from the tin and place it on a serving plate. Open the tin; the milk will have turned into toffee. Spread the contents evenly over the biscuit base. You will probably only need about half the tin, but it is up to you how much you use. Leave 3cm (1in) around the edge so the bananas don't slide off the pie. Pile the banana slices onto the pie so they cover the toffee.

Whip the cream into soft peaks using an electric whisk, adding the vanilla and sugar towards the end. Dollop the cream on top of the bananas and grate the chocolate over it. Yum.

Tip: You only need about half the tin of condensed milk, so the rest can be kept in an airtight container in the fridge and used as a toffee sauce. We like to heat it and then pour it over ice cream and bananas.

INDEX

Acknowledgements

A big THANK YOU to all:

Harriet Arbuthnot for being my right hand.

Sarah Canet for helping me wrestle the introduction into shape.

Alastair Laing for rolling up his sleeves and getting on with the job.

David Loftus for his vision.

Ned, my wonderful brother, for his charming drawings.

Sebastian and Gertrude for allowing us to invade their beautiful house and turn it into a pie laboratory.

Julian Biggs for his culinary alchemy.

Everyone at Portmeirion potteries, especially Julian Teed, for their support and encouragement.

Robin and Sian Llywelyn at Portmeirion for providing peace and calm at the wonderful village.

Grechen and Ewan at The Lacquer Chest for their stunning props.

Helena for keeping the kitchen spick-and-span, her big smiles and being top pie tester.

Lizzy Gray for her sweetness and cleverness.

And lastly, but not leastly, all my magnificent family and friends for their sensational recipes, support and pie-eating skills.

This edition first published in 2013 by HarperNonFiction.

This book includes recipes and images first published
in *Pies* by Sophie Conran, 2006.

HarperCollins*Publishers*
77–85 Fulham Palace Road
London W6 8JB

www.harpercollins.co.uk
www.harpercollins.com
10 9 8 7 6 5 4 3 2 1

Text © Sophie Conran 2006
Photography © David Loftus 2006
Design: Maru Studio
Editor: Alastair Laing
Food Stylist: Julian Biggs
Prop Stylist: Sophie Conran

A catalogue record for this book is available from the British Library.

ISBN: 978-0-00-749871-0

Printed and bound in China by RR Donnelley.